# The Hearing-Impaired Child in School

Edited by

**Raymond H. Hull, Ph.D.**

*Director of Audiology*
*Department of Communication Disorders*
*College of Health and Human Services*
*University of Northern Colorado*
*Greeley, Colorado*

**Karen L. Dilka, Ph.D.**

*Hearing Resource Teacher/Audiologist*
*Hearing Resource Program*
*Phoenix Union High School District*
*Phoenix, Arizona*

Grune & Stratton, Inc.
(Harcourt Brace Jovanovich, Publishers)

Orlando    San Diego    New York
London    Toronto    Montreal    Sydney    Tokyo

**Library of Congress Cataloging in Publication Data**
Main entry under title:

The hearing-impaired child in school.

   Bibliography.
   Includes index.
      1. Hearing-impaired children—United States—Addresses,
essays, lectures.   2. Mainstreaming in education—United
States—Addresses, essays, lectures.   I. Hull, Raymond H.
II. Dilka, Karen L.   [DNLM: 1. Education, Special.
2. Hearing disorders—In infancy and childhood.   3. Hearing
disorders—Rehabilitation..   WV 271 H435]
HV2437.H4      1984            371.91′2         84-4682
ISBN 0-8089-1663-7

**Grune & Stratton, Inc.**
*Orlando, FL 32887*

Distributed in the United Kingdom by
**Grune & Stratton, Ltd.**
*24/28 Oval Road, London NW 1*

Library of Congress Catalog Number 84-4682
International Standard Book Number 0-8089-1663-7
Printed in the United States of America

84  85  86  87     10  9  8  7  6  5  4  3  2  1

# Contents

# Preface

The purpose of this text is to present information that can be used by those who serve hearing-impaired children in the schools. It is intended to enhance the knowledge and efforts of those responsible for the schools that hearing-impaired children attend and the teachers who guide them through their academic learning experiences. It will also be useful to the hearing-impaired child's parents. *The Hearing-Impaired Child in School* is an ideal resource for educational and other specialists who serve hearing-impaired children in a school environment, as well as those who are preparing to become specialists. These include deaf educators, speech–language pathologists, social workers, nurses, physicians, and school audiologists.

The information in this book includes (1) the causes of hearing impairment in children; (2) hearing aids and other amplification devices that can enhance the function of hearing-impaired children in school; (3) placement and programming for hearing-impaired children in the school environment; (4) the roles of various professionals who work with hearing-impaired children in the schools and their interrelationships; (5) suggestions and procedures for mainstreaming hearing-impaired children into the schools; (6) the relationship between home and school in the development of hearing-impaired children; (7) language development procedures; (8) the identification and management of children who possess auditory processing disorders; (9) the roles and functions of various types of interpreters in a school environment, including philosophies and historical approaches; and (10) questions most frequently asked by parents and teachers of hearing-impaired children, and accurate responses to them.

This text fills a void in the literature as it relates to serving school-aged hearing-impaired children and their parents. It strives to strengthen the bond between teachers, parents, special educators, hearing specialists, and speech–language specialists in serving the needs of hearing-impaired children in school.

# Contributors

**Joyce Best, M.A.**   Teacher, Pre-School Program for the Acoustically Handicapped, Weld School District #6, University of Northern Colorado, Greeley, Colorado

**Linda K. Cleeland, M.A.**   Clinical Coordinator, Division of Audiology, Department of Communication Disorders, College of Health and Human Services, University of Northern Colorado, Greeley, Colorado

**Cheryl DeConde, Ed.D.**   Director of Educational Audiology Services, Weld School District #6, University of Northern Colorado, Greeley, Colorado

**Karen L. Dilka, Ph.D.**   Hearing Resource Teacher/Audiologist, Hearing Resource Program, Phoenix Union High School District, Phoenix Arizona

**J. Laurence Hayes, M.S.**   Department Chair, Interpreter Training Program, Pima Community College, Tucson, Arizona

**Raymond H. Hull, Ph.D.**   Director of Audiology, Department of Communication Disorders, College of Health and Human Services, University of Northern Colorado, Greeley, Colorado

**Rhonda E. Kaley, M.S., J.D.**   Assistant Professor of Audiology, Department of Communication Disorders, College of Health and Human Services, University of Northern Colorado, Greeley, Colorado

**Charlene M. Kampfe, Ph.D.**   Department of Rehabilitation and Counseling the Deaf, Department of Rehabilitation, University of Arizona, Tucson, Arizona

**Ron J. Leavitt, M.S.**   Clinic Coordinator, University of Arizona Adult and Child Hearing Clinics; Coordinator of Tucson Unified School District Audiology Services, University of Arizona, Tucson, Arizona

**Andrew Nielsen, M.A.**   Teacher, Program for the Acoustically Handicapped, Weld School District #6, University of Northern Colorado, Greeley, Colorado. Parent of a deaf son

**Sheryl L. Roesser, M.S.**   Speech-Language Pathologist, Program for the Acoustically Handicapped, Weld School District #6, University of Northern Colorado, Greeley, Colorado

*Raymond H. Hull*

# 1

# Addressing the Needs of the Hearing-Impaired Child

In November of 1975, Public Law 94–142 became law (Education for All Handicapped Children Act of 1975). Lauded as the "civil rights act for the handicapped," it was enacted as a result of the discovery that only about 50 percent of handicapped school-age children in the public schools were receiving the special educational services they needed. The Federal government determined that if school systems were not assuming their responsibility in providing adequate services to serve the special needs of handicapped children, then they would mandate it by Federal law.

Another law, which is called the Rehabilitation Act of 1973 (PL 93–112, Section 504), provides impaired students with the means in which to ensure, through legal channels if necessary, that they will not be prevented access to programs that receive Federal funds (Rehabilitation Act of 1973, 1973), including schools, colleges, and other programs where access by the handicapped is important. Those two laws have and continue to benefit the handicapped in school environments. In order to enforce the laws, if schools or other such agencies do not comply, the Federal government can remove or disallow Federal funds for which those schools have applied for program maintenance or for special projects.

One population of handicapped school-age children that these laws

THE HEARING-IMPAIRED CHILD IN SCHOOL
ISBN 0-8089-1663-7

have particularly assisted are the hearing impaired in school settings. Since hearing impairment is, in essence, an invisible disorder (that is, it is not as visibly observed as other handicaps), numerous hearing-impaired children either went undetected or unserved. Hearing impairment was among the easiest disorders to ignore, and potential programs for the hearing impaired were more likely to be set aside. That has been a tragic error in logic, since hearing-impaired students comprise the largest single population of school-age handicapped persons in the U.S. According to Ross, Brackett, and Maxon (1982), it is currently estimated that the percentage of children with educationally significant hearing losses "is in excess of 16 per 1000, probably much closer to 30 per 1000" (p. 3). That is equal to approximately 1.04 million children of school age, an extremely large population of children who are handicapped to varying degrees.

The purpose of this book is to address the needs of these children. The information is presented from the vantage point of professionals who have years of successful experience working with the hearing impaired of school age, in educational environments. The content is presented at a level that will be understandable to parents of hearing-impaired children and to regular educators who are responsible for hearing-impaired children who have been mainstreamed into their classroom. The text will be of interest to educators of the deaf who may desire information that will help to expand or clarify their current knowledge of various aspects of serving hearing-impaired children in the schools. Audiologists and speech-language pathologists in the schools who serve hearing-impaired children and their parents, and who provide counsel to regular educators as they serve mainstreamed children, can also benefit from this material.

This text not only presents information on types of hearing loss among school-age children and the provision of services on their behalf at school, but also on parental support of hearing-impaired children, assisting parents in helping their hearing-impaired children develop and maintain a sense of self-worth, self-confidence, and family membership. Suggestions for parents in providing language stimulation at home are included. The material in this text is an ideal resource for teachers, educators of the deaf, speech-language pathologists, audiologists, and parents.


## THE HEARING-IMPAIRED CHILD

Hearing loss that remains undetected, even during the first year of life after birth, can cause dramatic alterations in a child's potential for language and educational development. Without being seen, hearing loss robs children of academic achievements that otherwise they may have possessed the potential for. It robs them of the language and educational levels they may have otherwise gained, and the vocational, social, and personal achievements that may have accompanied them. Hearing loss results in a tragic waste of human potential, particularly when parents, teachers, and other professionals have not been provided information that will assist them in serving their child or their student. Thus, the purpose of this book.

Hearing-impaired children can be classified as the following:

1. The 16–30 percent of school-age children who possess hearing loss that is sufficiently significant to interfere with their ability to learn in school, or to develop language to their fullest potential.
2. The 10 percent of all children who fail tests of response to auditory stimuli at age 12 months.
3. The 1 in every 800–900 children in the U.S. who are deaf.
4. The 1.70 of all children who possess a significant hearing handicap at birth.
5. The approximate one child out of every 300 at early stages of development who cannot understand loud speech (Human Communication and Its Disorders, 1973.
6. The one in 10 to one in 16 who possess milder forms of hearing impairment that can handicap them in school.

The greatest detriment to those children who possess any level of hearing loss, from mild to profound, is that hearing impairment is an invisible handicap. It cannot be seen like the possible malformed eyes of a visually handicapped child, or the crippled limbs of the physically handicapped. It is, therefore, more difficult to identify at critical early ages.


## THE SUPPORTERS OF HEARING-IMPAIRED CHILDREN

Parents and teachers are perhaps the most influential in relation to the emotional, educational, and personal development of children. Those also include hearing-impaired children. Of course, audiologists, speech–language pathologists, and vocational rehabilitation counselors serve the hearing impaired, but they do not impact upon their total being as do their parents and teachers. For that reason, the content of this book is presented in such a way that extensive previous knowledge of the field of hearing is not necessary to comprehend it. Parents and teachers, along with professionals in the field who serve the hearing impaired will be able to share the information it contains on a more conversant basis.

## SERVICES FOR HEARING-IMPAIRED CHILDREN

The thrust of services on behalf of the hearing impaired have taken a positive turn in recent years. Rather than wasting precious time discussing or arguing the benefits and limitations of manualism versus oralism versus total communication, service providers are concentrating with greater energy on four important factors:

1. Earlier identification of hearing impairment;
2. Earlier fitting of amplification devices;
3. Earlier language stimulation programs that emphasize the needs of the child and the family as opposed to one person's strict philosophical approach;
4. Mainstreaming children whenever possible into a regular school setting while providing interpreter tutorial services and language stimulation programs.

These thrusts have existed for years. But, rather than being observed in isolated instances in demonstration programs, they are spreading across the U.S. and happily are becoming the rule rather than the exception. The content of this text concentrates on those important areas.

## THE ORGANIZATION OF THE TEXT

As stated in the Preface, the purpose of this text is to strengthen the bond between teacher, parent, and hearing specialist in serving hearing-impaired children in school. They deserve our best efforts; the more knowledgeable all who serve them are, the more completely hearing-impaired children will have the opportunity to develop educationally, socially, and personally.

As the text is read, the reader will recognize a sequence of informational events. For example, a concise discussion of the structure and function of the auditory system as they relate to a child's ability to hear and develop language is important for a fuller understanding of what can occur to disturb the function of the auditory system. That information is presented in Chapter 2. The sequence then leads the reader to Chapter 3, which provides a well-organized presentation on the various types of diseases and disorders that can affect children's hearing, and thus their ability to learn or to function communicatively.

Information on hearing aids and other amplifying devices is critical for an understanding of how they may or may not provide assistance for hearing-impaired children. Chapter 4 presents information on that topic.

As hearing-impaired children enter school, it is critical that those who serve them in that environment understand their role and the interrelationships of their role with others in the school environment, including administrators, teachers, special educators, health personnel, deaf educators, speech-language pathologists, and audiologists. That information is presented in Chapter 5. Chapter 7, then, presents an excellent discussion of the roles of those who serve the mainstreamed child in the regular school, and includes suggestions to teachers and administrators as mainstreamed children enter their school.

It is also imperative that those who serve hearing-impaired children in a school environment understand the processes, philosophies, and procedures for placement and programing for a most effective and rewarding learning experience. That is discussed in Chapter 6.

The relationships of home and school in the development of a positive self-image and the self-confidence necessary to succeed, not only in the school, but on the playground and other environments as well, have not been presented in the majority of texts on hearing-impaired children, particularly as they relate to language development. Yet, these relationships are critical in the development of all children, particularly in relation to children who are impaired to any degree. This important information is presented in Chapter 8.

As a companion to the above chapter, a specific discussion of the responsibilities and procedures for language development for hearing-impaired children is necessary to complete the intent of this book. That information is presented in Chapter 9 and was written by a successful and experienced speech–language pathologist whose professional position is centered in that arena.

Children who possess disorders of central auditory function will resemble, in some respects, children who are hearing impaired. It is important to understand what appears to cause the behaviors, what the behaviors are, and what can be done to serve those children. That discussion is presented in Chapter 10, specifically on causation, identification, and management.

As severely hearing-impaired children are mainstreamed into regular schools, the interpreter becomes an important part of the child's classroom life. The interpreter is there to assist the child in all aspects where a gap must be bridged between the person talking and the child's impaired hearing mechanism. The intricacies involved in the role of the interpreter are too many to be presented as a part of a chapter, so Chapter 11 is devoted to that important topic.

When parents are faced with the rearing of a hearing-impaired child, or when teachers find themselves in a position of having mainstreamed hearing-impaired children in their classroom, they generally find that they have questions that are sometimes difficult to find answers to. This is usually because books that discuss the areas in question are written at a technical level and are difficult for parents or teachers to understand, or the information is otherwise not readily available. The areas that parents and teachers have questions about most frequently revolve around heredity and hearing impairment, what syndromes are, what noise does to hearing, and oral versus manual communication. Chapter 12 is devoted to that discussion for parents and teachers.

Finally, there are many materials, books, language stimulation programs, and other resources that are available to teachers, parents, speech–language pathologists, deaf educators, and audiologists for use in their efforts on behalf of hearing-impaired children. In most instances, however, they are not compiled in one place for easy identification, including the addresses for ordering them. This information is presented at the conclusion of this book under the title, "Resource Materials For Use With Hearing-Impaired Children." The addresses for the materials are found in the last pages of that section.

This book is dedicated to hearing-impaired children in school, and to those who serve them. Its intent is to present informative discussions as opposed to theoretical information, on those children in the most understandable form.

## REFERENCES

*Education for All Handicapped Children Act of 1975.* Public Law 94-142. U.S. Congress, 94 Congress, First Session, U.S. Code, Section 1401–1461, 1975.
*Rehabilitation Act of 1973.* Section 504. Public Law 93-112. 29 U.S. Code, Section 706, 1973.
Ross, M., Brackett, D., & Maxon, A. Hard of hearing children in regular schools. In M. Ross, D. Brackett, & A. Maxon. *Hard of Hearing Children in Regular Schools.* Englewood Cliffs, New Jersey: Prentice-Hall, 1982, p.3.

*Linda Cleeland*

# 2

# The Function of the Auditory System in Speech and Language Development

## ANATOMY AND PHYSIOLOGY OF THE AUDITORY MECHANISM

The complexity of the human ear is truly phenomenal, particularly when one considers the minute size of many of the auditory structures. This small yet highly sophisticated system is composed of four main anatomical and functional areas: (1) the conductive mechanism, (2) the cochlea, (3) the auditory nerve, and (4) the central auditory system, including the auditory tracts through the brainstem and the higher auditory centers of the brain (see Fig. 2.1). By tracing the transmission of sound through the auditory system, a basis for understanding the anatomy and physiology of the auditory mechanism will be provided.

### The Conductive Mechanism

The conductive mechanism includes the pinna (auricle) or outer visible portion of the ear, the ear canal, the tympanic membrane or eardrum, and the middle ear structures (see Fig. 2-2). The purpose of

*This author would like to thank Lori Remegio for preparation of the illustrations presented in this chapter.*

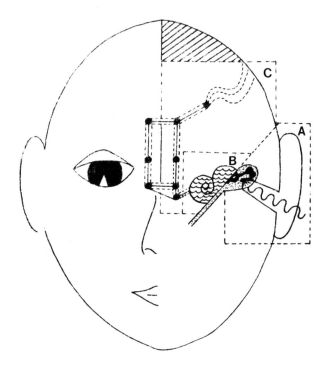

**Figure 2-1.** The auditory mechanism includes the (a)
conductive mechanism; (b) cochlea; and (c) auditory
nerve, brainstem auditory pathways, and auditory cortex.

this mechanism is to conduct sound from the environment to the inner
ear (cochlea). In man, the outer ear plays no functional role in audition
except in its resonating characteristics to high frequency sounds. The
ear canal, however, which is 1.25 inches long, directs airborne sound
waves toward the resilient tympanic membrane found at the end of the
slightly bent ear canal. The ear canal is also resonant to high frequency
sounds and functions to concentrate the energy of the acoustic signal
at the level of the tympanic membrane. The tympanic membrane vibrates
in response to the sound as sound waves reach it. This vibrating membrane continues the transmission of sound into the middle ear, a small
cavity adjacent to the tympanic membrane. The acoustical energy is
now no longer in the form of sound waves as a result of the level action
of the ossicular chain and its internal vibratory patterns. Instead, the
acoustical energy has been converted into mechanical energy as it continues through the middle ear. The vibrations are transmitted from the
tympanic membrane to the malleus, the first in a series of three small
bones that bridges across the middle ear space; the malleus is connected
to the tympanic membrane.

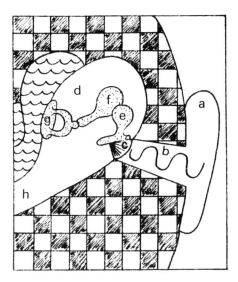

**Figure 2-2.** The conductive mechanism includes the (a) pinna, (b) ear canal, (c) tympanic membrane, (d) middle ear space, (e) malleus, (f) incus, (g) stapes, and (h) eustachian tube.

The energy will continue through this series of bones, the ossicular chain, vibrating the incus (the second bone in the series), and finally the stapes (the last bone in the chain). The ossicles are the smallest bones in the body and, as a chain they span approximately 0.25 inch (4–6 mm) across the middle ear space. As vibrations pass from the tympanic membrane through the middle ear, the relatively large size of the tympanic membrane in relationship to the base of the stapes results in a concentration of energy at the end of the ossicular chain. In addition, the ossicular chain functions as a lever with an "off-center" point of balance. This lever-like action, together with the size differential between the tympanic membrane and the stapes, amplifies the mechanical energy as it travels through the middle ear. The base of the stapes (the footplate) is positioned at the oval window, a membrane opening into the inner ear.

### The Sensory System and Auditory Nerves

The cochlea, or inner ear, is a coiled, fluid-filled tube having the shape of a snail; the total structure is smaller than the size of a pea (see

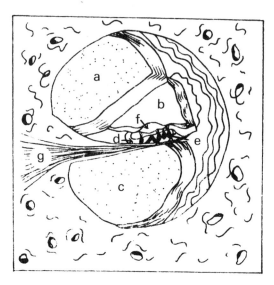

**Figure 2-3.** The cross section of a coil of the cochlea and organ of corti shows the (a) scala vestibuli; (b) scala media or cochlear duct; (c) scala tympani; (d) basilar membrane; (e) hair cells with projecting celia; (f) tectorial membrane; and (g) nerve fibers exiting hair cells and bundling.

Fig. 2-1 and Fig. 2-3). The cochlea houses the sensory cells of hearing. These cells, called hair cells, are part of a structure called the organ of Corti and are positioned along a supporting membrane—the basilar membrane. The organ of Corti and basilar membrane spiral through the full 1.50 inch length of the cochlea. The hair cells have fiber-like projections (cilia) that support the gelatinous tectorial membrane, a structure running parallel to the basilar membrane also through the full length of the cochlea. The cochlea receives the mechanical energy from the stapes as the stapes moves in the oval window. This stapedial movement activates cochlear fluid resulting in a wavelike motion of the basilar membrane. Hence, bending of the cilia occurs as the hair cells are displaced in relationship to the lagging tectorial membrane. Neuroelectrical impulses initiated from the shearing of the cilia against the tectorial membrane exit each sensory cell through nerve fibers at the base of the hair cells. The nerve fibers bundle to form the auditory branch of the VIIIth cranial nerve (see Fig. 2-3). The short path of the VIIIth nerve takes it through a bony opening into the cranial cavity where it immediately joins the brainstem. Therefore, the cochlea is truly an energy transducer that converts the vibrations transmitted through the middle

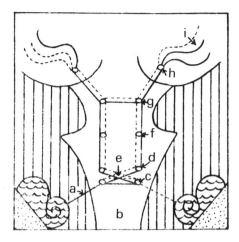

**Figure 2-4.** The auditory nerve is shown exiting the cochlea and entering the brainstem, with ascending auditory pathways and auditory cortex; (a) auditory nerve; (b) brainstem; (c) cochlear nuclei; (d) superior olivary complex; (e) trapezoid body—a tract of nerve fibers running horizontally from one side of the brainstem to the other; (f) nuclei of lateral lemniscus—an ascending auditory tract; (g) inferior colliculus; (h) medial geniculate body (at the level of the thalmus); and (i) auditory radiations to Heschl's gyrus in the temporal lobes of the cortex.

ear into electrical energy (nerve impulses) capable of traveling along specific neural tracts through the brainstem to Heschl's gyrus, the auditory cortex of the brain.

### The Brainstem Auditory Pathways and Auditory Cortex

As the nerve impulses from one ear enter the same side of the brainstem and begin to ascend along specific bundles of nerve fibers or pathways, they pass through, or terminate, in several well-delineated neuroanatomical junctions (see Fig. 2-4). These junctions are either synaptic sites between nerve cells where nerve impulses are passed from one nerve cell to another, or gatherings of nerve cell nuclei where some processing occurs. At these relay stations, portions of the neuroelectrical tracts terminate collectively, are re-routed, or continue their ascending routes (Beasley & Rintelmann, 1979). The function of the brainstem nuclei in regard to specific subskills of auditory processing includes roles in frequency and intensity discrimination, localization of sound, and analysis of time characteristics (Sanders, 1977). At certain brainstem nuclei along the auditory pathway, the auditory signals, now being transmitted as electrical signals, are routed across the midline to the opposite ascending pathway. Therefore, acoustical energy presented to only one ear will ultimately travel up both sides of the brainstem to the left and right hemispheres of the brain. When the nerve impulses reach the thalmus at the top of the brainstem, the auditory tracts fan out and enter the temporal lobes of the brain—the primary locations where auditory perception, interpretation, and storage occur. The auditory cortex includes both primary reception areas and association areas (Nolte, 1981).

## AUDITORY PERCEPTION OF SPEECH

Although auditory processing (the efficient use of the auditory information in the understanding of speech) is primarily a cortical event, each component of the auditory system plays a role in auditory perception of speech. A complex array of events occurs between the conductive mechanism where the signal first enters the auditory system and the central nervous system where sound is processed (see Fig. 2-5). Any disruption of these events can result in interruption of the processing of speech.

The normal conductive mechanism is capable of delivering high quality, unattenuated auditory signals to the inner ear. The cochlea not only serves to convert mechanical vibrations into electrical energy ca-

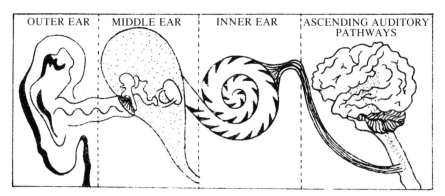

**Figure 2-5.**   Energy transduction through the auditory mechanism is detailed.

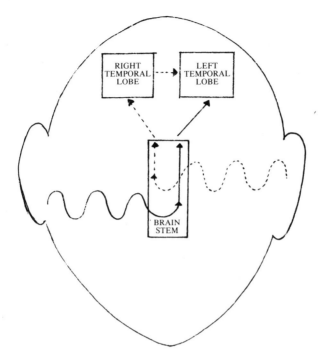

**Figure 2-6.** This figure shows the routing of linguistic information to the left hemisphere—the mechanism for the right ear advantage for speech processing (Speaks, 1975).

pable of traveling along the central auditory pathways, but it also codes and transmits the incoming signal according to the distinctive acoustical parameters of the original auditory stimulus, including intensity, frequency, and temporal (time) characteristics. Differing frequencies will result in maximum displacement of certain points of the basilar membrane, with high frequency information stimulating the base of the cochlea and progressively lower acoustical input affecting areas toward the apex of the cochlea. The corresponding nerve fibers exiting the basal hair cells will transmit the coded high frequency information, while the nerve fibers originating in the apex of the cochlea carry the low frequency energy. Intensity increases result in greater displacement of the basilar membrane, causing an increase in neural activity that results from additional shearing of the hair cells. Consequently, the exact nerve fibers that fire following acoustical stimulation and the number of fibers that fire are the cochlea's means of coding the information being channeled to the higher auditory centers.

It has been suggested (Speaks, 1975) that the left cerebral hemisphere is dominant usually in processing linguistic information. Auditory information arriving in the right auditory cortex goes through some preliminary analysis but is subsequently routed to the left hemisphere for detailed acoustical and linguistic analysis. Additionally, the right ear shows a listening advantage that is due, perhaps, to degradation of left ear stimuli, since it is channeled initially to the right cortex, then back to the left (see Fig. 2-6).

## Theories of Speech Perception in Speech–Language Development

What actually occurs at the various locations where auditory processing of linguistic information takes place continues to be a matter of theoretical speculation. Many models of speech perception have been suggested (Sanders, 1977). To facilitate the understanding of some of the subskills inherent in speech perception, Keir (1977) suggests a theoretical model that indicates that acoustical information, upon entering the central nervous system, collects in a short-term storage area. Higher processing levels sort and continue to process incoming meaningful information (i.e., meaningful speech) but reject the nonmeaningful signals, such as competing speech stimuli or noise. The short-term storage area serves, therefore, to separate and identify primary signals from competing background noise or nonmeaningful speech. This processing skill is called *auditory figure ground* and becomes important any time two or more auditory stimuli are being processed simultaneously. It allows the listener to attend to one of the signals. When one is exposed to speech that is comprised of familiar characteristics, a listener involuntarily perceives the familiar components of the stimuli. This automatic processing does not occur if the stimuli is unfamiliar and, thus, fails to trigger the involuntary processing mechanism (Stevens & House, 1972). For example, this is commonly experienced as we listen to, but fail to process, the words of someone who is speaking in a foreign language.

In the next stage of Keir's auditory perception model the coded, sequenced linguistic components of speech enter a short-term memory area. These segments of speech collect until they form a meaningful linguistic unit (meaningful words). Comparison of the incoming linguistic units with previously processed and stored information is a continuous process. When the new information is matched with stored information, an association is made, and the incoming coded message is recognized. Keir defines the process of associating the coded information with something stored in a long-term auditory memory as *auditory closure*. Acoustical information processed in short-term memory will be transferred into long-term memory where it can be stored but also scanned for association as new information enters the system. The shift from short-term to long-term memory makes way for new information entering the system.

Among normal young children, conventional linguistic rules and patterns that are fundamental to language learning are developing simultaneously in the same way as the child's skills in recognizing complex morphological signals (Bever, 1973). The combinations of speech sounds and their temporal relationships are learned through re-exposure and association as are the linguistic rules unique to language learning. Perception and processing of speech are also closely linked to our abilities to produce speech. Neural tracts connect the auditory association areas of the temporal lobe to the motor speech areas, allowing the speech perception mechanism and the speech production mechanism to coordinate tasks. Language acquisition is facilitated by revocalizing (saying) what is heard, thus activating neural connections between the speech reception and speech production areas (Tarnopol & Tarnopol, 1977).

The relative specificity of the functions of the brainstem auditory pathways and auditory cortex in processing information has been substantiated. A lesion in either of these areas of the central nervous system will not significantly impair hearing acuity or the detection of sound, but can result in an impairment of communication abilities as a listener tries to utilize speech in a meaningful way (Northern & Downs, 1978). With an abnormally functioning central auditory system or with any altering of the signal reaching the central auditory system, encountering barriers during language acquisition becomes a reality, and optimal utilization of auditory input is unlikely.

## Expected Auditory Behaviors

When auditory perception/reception of speech develops normally, the following behaviors in response to auditory stimulation can be expected:

### 1 Month
- will jump or startle in response to loud noises
- will begin to make gurgling sounds

### 3 Months
- will make babbling sounds
- will be aware of voices
- may quiet down to familiar voices close to ear
- stirs or awakens from sleep when there is a loud sound relatively close

## 6 Months

- makes vocal sounds when alone
- turns head toward sounds out of sight or when name is called and speaker is not visible
- vocalizes when spoken to directly

## 9 Months

- responds differently to a cheerful versus angry voice
- turns head toward sounds out of sight or when name is called and speaker is not visible
- tries to copy the speech sounds of others

## 12 Months

- can locate a sound source by turning head (whether the sound is at the side, above, or below ear level)
- ceases activity when parent's voice is heard
- recognizes own name
- uses single words correctly
- vocalizes emotions
- laughs spontaneously
- disturbed by nearby noises when sleeping
- attempts imitation of sounds and words
- understands some familiar phrases or words
- responds to music or singing
- increases babbling in type and amount

## 24 Months

- has more than 50 words in vocabulary
- uses two words together
- responds to rhythm of music
- uses voice for a specific purpose
- shows understanding of many phrases used daily in life
- plays with sound-making objects
- uses well-inflected vocalizations
- refers to himself/herself by name

## REFERENCES

Beasley, D.S., & Rintelmann, A.K. Central auditory processing. In W.F. Rintelmann (Ed.), *Hearing assessment*. Baltimore: University Park Press, 1979, pp. 321-349.
Bever, T.G. Language and perception. In G.A. Miller (Ed.).*Communication, language and meaning*. New York: Basic Books, Inc., 1973, pp. 149-158.

Keir, E.H. Auditory information processing and learning disabilities. In L. Tarnopol & M. Tarnopol (Eds.), *Brain function and reading disabilities*. Baltimore: University Park Press, 1977, pp. 147-175.

Nolte, J. *The human brain*. St. Louis: The C.V. Mosby Co., 1981.

Northern, J.L., & Downs, M.A. *Hearing in children*. Baltimore: Williams and Wilkins, 1978.

Sanders, D.A. *Auditory perception of speech*. Englewood Cliffs, New Jersey: Prentice-Hall, Inc., 1977.

Speaks, C.E. Dichotic listening: a clinical or research tool? In M. Sullivan (Ed.), *Central auditory processing disorders*. Omaha: University of Nebraska Medical Center, 1975, pp. 1-25.

Stevens, K., & House, A. Speech perception. In J. Tobias (Ed.), *Foundations of modern auditory theory, Vol. II*. New York: Academic Press, Inc., 1972, pp. 1-62.

Tarnopol, L., & Tarnopol, M. Introduction to neuropsychology. In L. Tarnopol & M. Tarnopol (Eds.), *Brain function and reading disabilities*. Baltimore: University Park Press, 1977, pp. 1-47.

*Cheryl DeConde*

# 3

# Hearing Impairment In School-Age Children

The language barrier that results from a severe hearing impairment can be one of the most devastating handicaps. Communication is the basis of our social and cognitive being; without it, growth and development is stymied, which in turn influences psychological, social, and intellectual processes. The partial or complete absence of hearing interferes with the development of these processes due to the absence of normal auditory input and the resultant effect on linguistic development.

## CAUSES OF HEARING IMPAIRMENT AMONG CHILDREN

Knowing the cause of a child's hearing impairment is not only helpful for management purposes, but it also provides resolution for the parents in addressing the problem. Unfortunately, a fairly large portion of children possess hearing impairment of unknown etiology. The 1970–1971 Annual Survey of Hearing-Impaired Children and Youth conducted by the Office of Demographic Studies at Gallaudet College, Washington, D.C., reported that 23.8 percent of hearing impairments present at birth and 14.2 percent of hearing impairments acquired after birth were due to unknown causes.

The following sections will deal with the most common hearing disorders found in children. Readers desiring more in-depth information should refer to Gerber and Mencher's *Auditory Dysfunction* (1980), Jaffe's *Hearing Loss in Children* (1977), and Northern and Downs' *Hearing in Children* (1978).

## Disorders of the Outer and Middle Ear

Disorders of the outer and middle ear typically cause conductive hearing impairment. A decrease in the loudness with which an air-conducted sound is detected by the auditory nerve is the result. Many of these disorders are associated with other craniofacial and skeletal abnormalities or syndromes. A visible irregularity of the outer ear or ear canal is an immediate indication that hearing ability should be investigated; additionally, a prenatal and birth history should be conducted in search of other possible defects.

Types of disorders of the outer and middle ear are listed below.

### Outer Ear

*Microtia* of the outer ear, the pinna, refers to an abnormality in its size and shape. Most often the pinna is quite small and misshapen or may be totally absent. When the ear canal is completely closed off, *atresia* exists, while *stenosis* refers to the narrowing of the ear canal. Atresia and stenosis may occur with or without microtia. *Cerumen*, or ear wax, can become impacted in the ear canal so that its blockage causes a mild hearing loss. For most people the ear's self-cleaning system naturally moves the wax out of the ear so that it can be wiped with a washcloth; for others, it is necessary to have the cerumen removed by a physician. A cotton-tipped applicator can create more problems than it may remedy and should never be inserted into the ear canal.

*Foreign bodies* such as small rocks, corn kernels, thistles, or cereal are common objects removed from children's ears.

Fungal and bacterial infections of the skin of the external ear canal are called *otitis externa* and usually are manifested in an inflammation of this area. A common cause of this disorder is water left in the ear canal after swimming or bathing. Hearing aid users also are more prone to otitis externa as a result of the earmold of the hearing aid occluding the ear canal, thereby trapping moisture in the canal space. Otitis externa is not usually accompanied by hearing impairment.

### Middle Ear

The most common disorder of the middle ear is *middle ear effusion*. This term refers to the various conditions of fluid that may exist in this space; it has been estimated to affect as many as 30 percent of all 2-

year-olds, when it is most prevalent, declining to 15 percent by 11 years (Kessner, Snow, & Singer, 1974). *Otitis media* further describes this disorder and is differentiated into several categories:

SEROUS OTITIS MEDIA.    The presence of clear fluid in the middle ear is usually a result of the negative pressure created by the malfunction of the eustachian tube. Hearing levels vary but are often essentially normal, so that tympanometry or pnuematic otoscopy is necessary to identify the disorder.

ACUTE OTITIS MEDIA.    This term describes an "ear infection," the painful inflammation of the tympanic membrane (eardrum) and the middle ear. The pain from this inflammation is relieved often by the rupture of the tympanic membrane because of the pressure created by the fluid in the middle ear. The pus-like discharge may appear on the child's pillow or may drain from the ear. These small perforations heal spontaneously, usually. Hearing levels vary depending on the amount and viscosity of the fluid. Tympanometry is abnormal.

CHRONIC OTITIS MEDIA.    This term is used for a middle ear disease of long-standing duration that is associated usually with a perforation of the tympanic membrane and consequent pus-like discharge from the middle ear space. This is differentiated from *recurrent otitis media* where the middle ear returns to normal between episodes. Often the associated hearing loss is significant, with the degree dependent upon the extent of the disease process. Sensori-neural hearing loss can also occur as a result of this disorder. Tympanometry is abnormal.

Other side effects of middle ear effusion include scarring to the tympanic membrane as a result of eardrum ruptures and the consequent thickening of the tympanic membrane tissue as it heals, tympano-sclerotic plaque, and monomeric membranes. *Mastoiditis* is an acute inflammation of the mastoid air cells of the temporal bone and may follow severe acute bacterial otitis media. Deep pain and tenderness, including a foul–smelling discharge, are often present, and surgery may be necessary to clean out the diseased area. Hearing can be restored to normal following the surgery but may be permanently damaged depending on the extent of the disease process.

BULLOUS MYRINGITIS.    Bullous myringitis, a blister on the eardrum that often occurs as part of an upper respiratory infection, is manifested by sudden, severe pain of the ear.

*Ossicular Chain*

Usually abnormalities of the ossicular chain occur in children as a result of birth defects, but they may be present from disease also (middle ear effusion or the early stages of otosclerosis), or trauma such as a blow to the head. Growing skin from the ear canal can enter the middle ear space to form a growth called a *cholesteatoma* that can erode the ossicles or otherwise damage middle ear structures as part of the disease process. Hearing loss is associated with the above disorders with the exception of bullous myringitis.

## Sensori–Neural Hearing Impairment

Sensori-neural hearing loss refers to the impaired sensitivity to sound resulting from abnormalities of the cochlea, the sensory receptor for sound, and the auditory nerve. The degree of hearing impairment is a direct function of the amount of damage to these delicate hair cells and nerve fibers, varying from a mild hearing loss to total absence of hearing. Some impairments are progressive or do not appear until some point after birth. Causes of sensori-neural hearing loss may be divided into two categories: *genetic* and *nongenetic*.

### Genetic

Approximately 50 percent of childhood hearing impairment is inherited with more than 50 types of hereditary causes reported (Rose, Conneally, & Nance, 1977). Most of these hearing impairments occur with other anomalies and are usually part of a syndrome. Genetic traits may be transmitted through dominant, recessive, or sex–linked means.

A person with *autosomal dominant* genetic deafness has a 50 percent chance of passing it on to each of his or her offspring. The term autosomal refers to the placement of the abnormal gene on one of the pairs of nonsex chromosomes. Dominantly inherited traits vary in the degree to which the characteristic appears; in this case the degree of penetrance would determine the degree of hearing loss. Alport's syndrome, Waardenberg's syndrome, and Treacher–Collins syndrome are among the examples of this type of deafness that accounts for about 15 percent of all childhood hearing loss (Fraser, 1964).

Children with *autosomal recessive* genetic deafness, in contrast to the dominant type, have parents who carry the trait but are asymptomatic. For the trait to appear, both parents must carry the same recessive trait; 25 percent of their offspring will demonstrate the trait, 50 percent will be carriers, and 25 percent will be genetically normal. Recessive traits tend to occur with greater severity than dominant ones, and they cause about 40 percent of childhood deafness. Intermarriages within families increase the likelihood of recessive genetic defects. Pendred's syndrome and Usher's syndrome are recessive disorders with accompanying hearing impairment.

Sex-linked genetic deafness occurs as a result of genes located on the X chromosome. A female carrier has a 50 percent chance that each of her sons will be affected and a 50 percent chance that each of her daughters will be carriers. The trait cannot be passed from father to son, but all of the daughters of an affected male are carriers. Hearing impairment as a result of this type of genetic aberration accounts for about 2 percent of hearing loss in children, may occur with or without other associated abnormalities, and may vary in the degree of hearing loss.

*Nongenetic*

Nongenetic sensori-neural hearing impairments may be a result of prenatal, birth, or postnatal factors. Hearing loss results when bacterial,

**Table 3-1**  *Summary of Known Exogenous Causes of Prelingual Deafness**

Preconception and Prenatal Causes

Rubella
Cytomegalovirus
Ototoxic and other drugs, maternal alcoholism
Hypoxia (and its possible causes: high altitude, general anesthetic, severe hemorrhage)
Syphilis
Toxemia, diabetes, other severe systemic maternal illness
Parental irradiation
Toxoplasmosis

Perinatal Causes

Hypoxia
Traumatic delivery
Maternal infection
Ototoxic drugs
Premature delivery

Neonatal and Postnatal Causes

Hypoxia
Infection
Ototoxic drugs
Erythroblastosis fetalis
Infantile measles or mumps
Otitis media (acute, chronic, serous)
Noise-induced
Meningitis
Encephalitis

*Reproduced from Bergstrom, L., Hemenway, W. O. & Downs, M. P. A high risk registry to find congenital deafness. *Otolaryngol Clin North Am*, 1971, *4*, 369–399. With permission.

viral, or other toxic substances invade the inner ear structures via the bloodstream or from the cranial pathways. Trauma, lack of oxygen, and Rh incompatibility are other common causes of hearing impairment. Bergstrom, Hemenway, and Downs (1971) have summarized the major nongenetic causes of hearing loss, presented in Table 3-1.

PRENATAL INFECTIONS.    Infection during pregnancy is the major source of congenital deafness that is not hereditary. Rubella, contracted by the mother during pregnancy, represents the largest known prenatal cause of hearing impairment due to the epidemic of the mid 1960s. Although hearing loss may result from infection at any point during pregnancy, the first trimester is the most critical, where deafness occurs in 68 percent of those infected. This is reduced to 40 percent in the second trimester. Hearing loss is usually moderately severe to profound. Other associated abnormalities include heart defects in 50 percent of the population, cataract or glaucoma (40 percent), and psychomotor retardation (40 percent) (Cooper, 1969). Cytomegalic inclusion disease, a syndrome that often includes hearing impairment, is identified by low birth weight, jaundice, enlarged kidney and spleen, inflammation of the retina, anemia, and microcephaly. Toxoplasmosis is another major prenatal infection that leads to a higher incidence of hearing loss with symptoms similar to those of cytomegalic inclusion disease.

DRUGS.    Certain drugs taken during pregnancy can result in hearing loss in the newborn infant. These are referred to as ototoxic drugs and include streptomycin, dihydrostreptomycin, kanamycin, neomycin, and ethacrynic acid. Obviously their use is scrutinized closely.

BIRTH ABNORMALITIES.    Abnormalities at birth that may cause sensori-neural hearing impairment include anoxia (lack of oxygen) and birth trauma, low birth weight, and hyperbilirubinemia and kernicterus. With the latter as well as with Rh incompatibility, the incidence has been reduced dramatically due to medical treatment of the problem. The hearing loss associated with these disorders is most pronounced usually in the high frequencies.

MENINGITIS AND ENCEPHALITIS.    Meningitis and encephalitis are the two major infections affecting infants that cause hearing loss. Depending on the type of meningitis contracted, the resulting handicaps also include mental retardation, abnormal speech, motor delay, and seizures. Viral encephalitis is often fatal in newborns and in those who survive results in severe neurologic involvement including retardation.

## Central Auditory Processing Disorders

The central auditory pathways carry acoustic information via the auditory nerve to the cortex of the brain where interpretation and meaning are determined. The integration of signals from both ears and the complexity of the neurologic pathways yield a highly efficient system. Any malfunction or disturbance to this system can lead to varying degrees of auditory, speech, language, and learning problems. An in-depth discussion of central auditory processing disorders can be found in Chapter 10.

## THE SIGNIFICANCE OF HEARING IMPAIRMENT

The amount of residual hearing has a direct impact on a child's speech and language development, social–emotional stability, and academic performance. Obviously the greater the hearing loss, the greater the disability. There are also several other factors, such as intelligence, age of onset of the hearing loss, age of identification, economic factors, and parental support, which may lessen or increase the impact of the hearing impairment.

## The Effect of Mild (15–40dB) and Moderate (40–65dB) Hearing Loss

Children with hearing loss in these categories are often difficult to identify and, in fact, may not be detected until the child is part of a routine hearing screening program, usually when he/she enters kindergarten. These children appear to respond to auditory stimuli often enough, even though inconsistently, that a hearing problem may not be suspected. Children with mild and moderate hearing impairment may have good articulation and language ability even though they have difficulty hearing many speech sounds, faint or distant speech, and group conversation. They appear to "get by" in the regular classroom, although there is often a gap between their performance and their ability. By third or fourth grade the seemingly inconsequential problems of the past have now emerged in a significant concern, which not only affects their academic performance, but also their social–emotional stability. The children with mild and moderate losses, and some of those with severe losses, find that they do not fit in with the deaf students nor do they mingle easily with the normal hearing students. They are hard of hearing, a group for which there has been little concern in the past. This group of students has a unique style of learning and a greater incidence of social–emotional problems, which are only two of the characteristics that educators of the deaf have identified and are now grappling with.

Insecurity and paranoia are two behaviors common in this group of children. These problems stem from the partial hearing of conversation or instruction necessitating these students to speculate constantly and to fill in information in order to respond appropriately. For many students this becomes a tedious and frustrating task, so much so that a child who lacks the necessary perseverance and self-confidence gives up easily and withdraws from the situation. Younger children often appear inattentive or distracted because the input they receive auditorially is so difficult to sort out unless it is received under optimal listening conditions. Because these children communicate orally and appear to function on the surface as normal hearing youngsters, the expectations placed on them have generally been unreasonable. To combat potential social and emotional problems, identification and treatment of the impairment and subsequent consultation with the child, teachers, parents, and other persons involved must occur so that there is a clear understanding of the communication and learning processes under which the child will best function.

### The Effect of Minimal Auditory Deficiency

A syndrome in its own right, minimal auditory deficiency plagues millions of children during their toddler and preschool years. Minimal auditory deficiency is typically the result of the hearing loss associated with otitis media, which is the largest cause of mild and moderate hearing loss in children. When this condition persists or recurs, the cumulative effect of the reduced hearing may yield a significant decrease in learning ability. The 1977–1978 Annual Survey of Hearing-Impaired Children and Youth by the Office of Demographic Studies at Gallaudet College in Washington, D.C., reported otitis media as the cause in 76.5 percent of all hearing impairments less than or equal to 70 decibels (dB). Table 3-2 summarizes the causes of hearing impairment by degree of loss as reported in this survey.

The traditional criterion for minimal or mild hearing loss has been 26dB. However, research during the decade of the 1970s identified overwhelmingly the educational significance of a 15dB hearing loss when associated with middle ear pathology (Boyd, 1974; Downs, 1975, 1976; Eisen, 1962; Holm & Kunze, 1969; Howie, in Jaffe, 1977; Kaplan, Fleshman, & Bender, 1973; Katz, 1978; Lewis, 1976; Ling, 1972; Needleman, in Jaffe, 1977; Northern & Downs, 1978; Quigley, 1970; Skinner, 1978). Studies (Katz & Epstein, 1962; Katz, 1978 and Webster & Webster, 1977) have shown that conductive hearing loss is more than

**Table 3-2** Percent Distributions of Hearing Loss for Various Probable Causes of Hearing Impairment*

| | Reported Cause | | | | | | | | | | | | | |
| | At Birth or Congenital | | | | | | After Birth | | | | | | | |
| Degree of Hearing Loss (BEA—better ear average) | Maternal Rubella | Pregnancy Complications | Heredity | Trauma at Birth | Prematurity | Rh Incompatibility | Mumps | Measles | Meningitis | High Fever | Infection | Otitis Media | Trauma after Birth | Cause Cannot Be Determined |
|---|---|---|---|---|---|---|---|---|---|---|---|---|---|---|
| Less than Severe (70 dB) | 15.7 | 31.7 | 27.4 | 31.9 | 31.5 | 29.2 | 44.7 | 29.5 | 17.6 | 32.6 | 57.9 | 76.5 | 41.1 | 30.7 |
| Severe (71–90 dB) | 30.7 | 25.6 | 22.8 | 29.0 | 29.7 | 29.8 | 17.8 | 28.4 | 21.2 | 24.7 | 17.9 | 10.5 | 22.9 | 24.4 |
| Profound (91 dB) | 53.7 | 42.7 | 49.7 | 39.0 | 38.9 | 41.0 | 37.4 | 42.1 | 61.2 | 42.7 | 24.3 | 13.0 | 36.1 | 44.8 |
| Total number and percent of Annual Survey sample reporting cause | 8,966 (17.5) | 1,440 (2.8) | 4,597 (9.0) | 1,109 (2.2) | 1,952 (3.8) | 1,036 (2.0) | 219 (0.4) | 662 (1.3) | 3,205 (6.3) | 1,409 (2.7) | 1,125 (2.2) | 944 (1.8) | 137 (0.3) | 13.974 (25.8) |

In some cases, more than one cause was reported for a student.
*Reproduced from Karchmer, M., Milone, M., & Wolk, S. Educational significance of hearing loss at three levels of severity. Am Ann Deaf, 1979, Vol 124, 101. With permission.

just a blockage of sound to the hearing sensory organ. Rather, sensory deprivation occurs from the reduction in sound to the nerve, which results in an altered physiological response and development of the central nervous system. According to Katz (1978), aberrant development of the central nervous system function is likely if deprivation occurs early in life and over a period of time. The hearing loss can adversely affect the development of language and the development of auditory perceptual skills, therefore, increasing the likelihood of the presence of a significant learning disability. Otitis media obviously requires comprehensive detection methods and vigorous treatment and follow up. Typical pure-tone hearing screenings are conducted at 20dB to 25dB. Unless they include tympanometry (a specific test of middle ear function), otitis media is not detected in about 50 percent of the cases Cohen & Saad, 1972; DeConde, 1977; Eagles, Wishik, & Doerfler, 1967; McCandless & Thomas, 1974).

Why is 15dB hearing loss so detrimental and how does it affect the development of language? According to Northern and Downs (1978) and Skinner (1978), the amount of energy individual speech sounds produce varies. The voiced vowels and consonants carry the majority of the energy, while the unvoiced consonants such as s,p,t,k,th,f, and sh contain little. In normal rapid conversational speech, a normal hearing person may not even hear these sounds but is able to fill in what is missed because the strategies necessary for understanding speech and language have been developed. In a child just learning these skills, however, it is necessary to hear all sounds clearly in order to develop the perceptions and relationships adequately. Therefore, the greatest impact of otitis media, its associated hearing loss, and its effect on language and learning is when it occurs during the first 2 years of life.

Several studies (Eisen, 1962; Holm & Kunze, 1969; Kaplan, Fleshman, & Bender, 1973; Katz & Ullmer, 1972; Needleman, 1977) have reported the learning and consequent achievement delays in children who have had otitis media. Spelling, phonics, reading, verbal expression, and any tasks involving the receiving and processing of auditory stimuli are the most common skills affected.

Of paramount importance to this issue is the need for early detection and intervention of otitis media. Physicians must be better informed as to the educational implications of mild hearing loss in young children, as they are the primary health care professionals involved consistently in their management. Parents, and health and educational professionals, must be aware also of the ramifications in order to develop intervention programs to minimize the effects of auditory deprivation as well as to understand the needs of the child who has experienced this disorder.

## The Effect of Severe (65–90dB) and Profound (90dB+) Hearing Loss

Children with severe and profound hearing impairments represent the largest portion of students served in deaf education programs in this country. Table 3-3 describes the distribution of students served based on the 1977–1978 Annual Survey. It is interesting to note that, although the incidence of mild and moderate hearing impairments in children is seven times greater than that of severe and profound, the reported number of students served is more than 2:1 in favor of the severe/profound group. Obviously there are a great deal of mild and moderately hearing-impaired students who are not being served in special education programs. The Survey found direct correlations with the degree of hearing impairment and the educational placement (the greater the impairment the more restrictive the setting), speech intelligibility (the greater the loss, the poorer the rating of intelligibility), communication system used (the greater the loss, the higher likelihood of the use of sign), and hearing aid usage (highest among students with moderate and severe losses).

**Table 3-3** *Frequency and Percent Distributions of Hearing Loss for Students in the 1977–78 Annual Survey of Hearing Impaired Children and Youth\**

|  | Frequency (N) | Percent (%) |
|---|---|---|
| Total number of students in Annual Survey | 54,080 | 100.0 |
| Number of students for whom audiological data were not reported or were incomplete | 2,818 | 5.2 |
| Total known data (better ear average) | 51,262 | 100.0 |
| Normal (less than 27dB) | 2,250 | 4.4 |
| Mild (27–40dB) | 2,743 | 5.4 |
| Moderate (41–55dB) | 4,536 | 8.8 |
| Moderately severe (56–70dB) | 6,640 | 13.0 |
| Severe (71–90dB) | 12,666 | 24.7 |
| Profound (91dB or greater) | 22,427 | 43.7 |

\*Reproduced from Karchmer, M., Milone, M., & Wolk, S. Educational significance of hearing loss at three levels of severity. *Am Ann Deaf*, 1979, *124*, 98. With permission.

Oral speech skills are limited in this population because normal conversational speech occurs at a softer intensity than can be heard. Amplification through hearing aids and FM auditory systems enable the loudness level of conversation to be increased, but it does not correct the distortion that is inherent as a result of the nerve damage. Even with intensive speech, language, and auditory stimulation and therapy, use of total communication is necessary to ensure that information can be maximally understood.

Academically, these students are often behind their peers, with reading ability the most common skill affected. The language barrier seems to be the primary mitigating factor causing the depressed performance. As a result of this deficit, sign systems based on the semantic and syntactic structure of language, rather than the conceptual aspect, have evolved. Recent data on the Stanford Achievement Test taken by high school hearing-impaired students has shown that students who used the Seeing Essential English sign system (one of semantic and syntactic translation) performed much higher than students not using this system.

Social–emotional problems in deaf children have been influenced by certain factors that are inherent to this population. Those include the etiology of the hearing impairment and the incidence of associated disorders, the fact that 90 percent of hearing-impaired children are born to hearing parents (Schein & Delk, 1974), and the lack of psychologists who are trained to work with the deaf. Hearing-impaired students represent a heterogenous population, as do normal students. The impetus of educators must be to better understand the psychosocial development of the hearing impaired so that preventive measures can be implemented to address issues before they become problems.

## The Effect of Unilateral and High Frequency Hearing Loss

Recent attention has been given to children with unilateral and high frequency hearing losses. Factors that influence the degree of handicap that may result include whether the loss is in the right or left ear for unilateral impairments, the severity of the loss, and the age at onset of the loss. For unilateral impairments it has been reported that children who have right ear hearing function better than children whose left ear is their better ear (Bess, 1983). Similar learning problems as found in those children with minimal auditory deficiency may also occur in this population. A major difficulty experienced by these students is a reduced ability to understand speech when there is background noise present. Social–emotional concerns are also evident. Further study is necessary to evaluate carefully the various skills of these children.

## OTHER FACTORS INFLUENCING THE DEVELOPMENT OF THE HEARING-IMPAIRED CHILD

Many factors, in addition to the degree of hearing impairment, affect the total development of the child. Some of these are discussed below.

1. *Associated impairments.* Hearing-impaired children often exhibit neurological or other physical deficiencies as part of the etiology. The resultant behaviors may influence the child's attention skills, visual abilities, motor development, or perceptual skills. An example is a child who has had meningitis who, in addition to hearing loss, may have neurological deficiencies causing inattentiveness, seizures, and occasional abusive behavior. Table 3-4 provides data from the 1977–1978 Annual Survey indicating the distribution of various additional handicaps in relation to the degree of hearing impairment.

2. *Intelligence.* The child's intellectual abilities greatly influence the rate of learning and, of course, the learning potential. Intelligence testing also provides insight as to the student's strong and weak ability areas. With hearing-impaired and deaf children, intellectual measures must be done using instruments that are either normed on the deaf or that consist of nonverbal measures.

3. *Early identification and intervention.* The earlier the handicap is identified and treatment begun, the greater the potential for the child. Constant language input enhanced with amplification and sign language must occur in infancy if the child is to be given optimal opportunity for normal development.

4. *Parental acceptance and support.* Parental acceptance of the hearing handicap is as critical as early identification. Without their cooperation, intervention programs cannot provide enough support to be successful. Children are able to sense the ease with which their parents interact with them. Happy children are ones who know their parents are proud of them as they are.

5. *Social and economic factors.* These factors should not influence the development of the child if the same opportunities and programs are available for all children. Social and cultural differences may affect family priorities, however, so that a child does not receive the necessary support at home. Programs are available throughout the country that provide funding for hearing aids and therapy programs for low-income families. The assurance that the parents will follow through with these programs is more dependent on their commitment than on their financial ability. A comparison of the distribution of hearing loss of individuals from four ethnic

**Table 3-4**  *Percent Distributions of Hearing Loss for Specific Handicapping Conditions*\*

| | Handicapping Conditions | | | | | | | | |
|---|---|---|---|---|---|---|---|---|---|
| Degree of Hearing Loss (BEA) | Visual Impairment | Brain Damage | Epilepsy | Orthopedic | Cerebral Palsy | Heart Disorder | Mental Retardation | Emotional/ Behavioral Problem | Specific Learning Disability |
| Less than Severe (≤70dB) | 33.1 | 36.2 | 32.3 | 32.7 | 28.9 | 26.4 | 42.8 | 28.3 | 54.2 |
| Severe (71–90dB) | 26.9 | 25.8 | 20.8 | 25.5 | 31.0 | 28.6 | 22.4 | 24.5 | 20.3 |
| Profound (≥91dB) | 40.0 | 38.0 | 46.9 | 41.8 | 40.1 | 45.0 | 34.8 | 47.1 | 25.5 |
| Total number and percent of Annual Survey sample with each handicapping condition | 3,789 (7.4) | 1,333 (2.6) | 461 (0.9) | 966 (1.9) | 1,460 (2.9) | 1,313 (2.6) | 4,008 (7.8) | 3,421 (6.7) | 801 (1.6) |

In some cases, more than one additional handicapping condition was reported for a student.

*Reproduced from Karchmer, M., Milone, M., & Wolk. S. Educational significance of hearing loss at three levels of severity. Am Ann Deaf, 1979, Vol. 124, 104. With permission.

**Table 3-5** *Frequency and Percent Distributions of Hearing Loss by Ethnic Background, 1977–1978**

|  | Ethnic Background | | | | | | | |
|  | White | | Black | | Hispanic | | Other | |
| Degree of Hearing Loss (BEA) | N | (%) | N | (%) | N | (%) | N | (%) |
| Less than Severe (≤70dB) | 10,948 | (31.7) | 2,494 | (29.7) | 1,368 | (31.7) | 379 | (31.0) |
| Severe (71–90dB) | 8,417 | (24.4) | 2,158 | (25.7) | 1,071 | (24.8) | 283 | (23.2) |
| Profound (≥91dB) | 15,122 | (43.8) | 3,735 | (44.5) | 1,877 | (43.5) | 560 | (45.8) |
| Total number and percent of Annual Survey sample for each ethnic group | 34,487 | (71.2) | 8,387 | (17.3) | 4,316 | (8.9) | 1,222 | (2.5) |

Excluded from this table are 5,668 students for whom audiological or ethnic information was not reported.

*Reproduced from Karchmer, M., Milone, M., & Wolk, S. Education significance of hearing loss at three levels of severity. *Am Ann Deaf*, Vol. 124, 1979, April, 103. With permission.

backgrounds to degree of hearing loss (based on the 1977–1978 Annual Survey) is shown in Table 3-5.

## Severity Scale for Hearing Impairment

It is often helpful to consider objectively the capabilities of the child when determining service delivery systems in school. The scale shown in Figure 3-1 was designed to aid in that process. The scale incorporates many of the contributing factors that have been discussed in this chapter.

**Figure 3-1.**   Severity Scale for Hearing Impairment.

NAME _____   ASSESSMENT DATE: _____
D.O.B.:/AGE: _____   AUDIOLOGIST: _____

Directions: Circle appropriate points for each category.
   I.   *Degree of Hearing Loss*

      A.   Hearing Level—better ear (P.T.A. 500,1K,2K)

          0.0   normal (0–15dB)
          1.0   mild (15–40dB)
          2.0   moderate (40–65dB)
          3.0   severe (65–90dB)
          4.0   profound (90dB+)

      B.   Additional Factors:

          1.0   fluctuating hearing levels/progressive hearing loss

          If hearing level above is normal (0), add for the following:

          0.5   unilateral high frequency—mild to moderate (15–65dB)
               (H.F.P.T.A. 2K,4K,8K)
          1.0   unilateral high frequency—severe to profound (65dB+)
          1.5   bilateral high frequency—mild to moderate/unilateral
               profound
          2.0   bilateral high frequency—severe to profound (65dB+)

          Score _____

  II.   *Age of Onset*

          0.0   7 years or later
          1.0   postlingual (3–7 years)
          2.0   18 months–3 years
          3.0   3–18 months
          4.0   birth–3 months

          Score _____

III. *Auditory Discrimination Ability* (Unaided Sound Field @ 55dBHL or 30dBSL in quiet—PBK or WIPI)

    0.0  80–100%
    1.0  60–80%
    2.0  40–60%
    3.0  20–40%
    4.0   0–20%

    Score _____

IV. *Aided Auditory Ability*

A. In quiet (Sound Field @ 55dBHL or 30dBSL—PBK or WIPI)

    0.0  80–100%
    1.0  60–80%
    2.0  40–60%
    3.0  20–40%
    4.0   0–20%

B. With background noise (cafeteria or white noise (0 S/N) Sound Field @ 55dBHL or 30dBSL—PBK or WIPI)

    0.0  80–100%
    0.5  60–80%
    1.0  40–60%
    1.5  20–40%
    2.0   0–20%

    Score _____

V. *Contributing Factors* (add for problems in following areas)

    1.0  central auditory processing skills/neurological functioning
    0.5  vision
    0.5  social/emotional
    0.5  bilingualism
    0.5  motivation
    0.5  mental age/I.Q.
    0.5  chronological age
    0.5  home environment
    0.5  other medical
    0.5  communication ability
    0.5  language ability
    0.5  speech-reading ability

    Score _____

Total Score I–IV: _____

Contributing Factors V: _____

Total: _____ ÷ 4 = Severity Rating _____

*Rating Guidelines*

0.0–1.0 no services

Minimum points =    .5–score = .125

1.0–2.0 questionable/mild needs

Maximum points = 27.5 – score – 6.875

2.0–3.0 moderate needs

3.0 → severe needs

*Comments*

# REFERENCES

Bergstrom, W., Hemenway, W.G., & Downs, M.P. A high risk registry to find congenital deafness. *Otolaryngol Clin North Am*, 1971, 4, 369-399.

Bess, F. *Children with unilateral hearing loss.* Paper presented at *Colorado Speech and Hearing Association* annual meeting, Colorado Springs, May, 1983.

Bess, F., & McConnell, F. *Audiology, education, and the hearing impaired child.* St. Louis, Missouri; C.V. Mosby, 1981.

Boyd, S.F. *Hearing loss; its educationally measureable effects of achievement.* Masters thesis, Southern Illinois University, Carbondale, 1974.

Cohen, C., & Saad, J. Hearing in secretory otitis media. *Can J Otolaryngol*, 1972, 1, 27.

Cooper, L.Z., et al. Rubella; clinical manifestations and management. *Am J Disabled Child*, 1969, 118, 18.

DeConde, C. Tympanometry in school screening programs. Weld County School Dsitrict #6, Greeley, Colorado. Unpublished paper. 1977.

Downs, M.P. Hearing loss: definition, epidemiology and prevention. *Public Health Review*, 1975, 4, 225-380.

Downs, M.P. The handicap of deafness. In J.L. Northern (Ed.), *Hearing disorders.* Boston: Little, Brown, & Co., 1976.

Eagles, E.L., Wishik, S.M., & Doerfler, L.G. Hearing sensitivity and ear disease in children: a prospective study. *Laryngoscope* (Monograph 1-274), 1967.

Eisen, N.H. Some effects of early sensory deprivation on later behavior; the quondum hard of hearing child. *J Abnorm Social Psychol*, 1962, 65, 338-342.

Fraser, G.R. Profound childhood deafness. *J Med Genet* 1964, 1, 118-151.

Gerber, S.E., & Mencher, G. *Auditory dysfunction.* Houston: College-Hill Press, 1980.

Holm, V.A., & Kunze, L.H. Effect of chronic otitis media on language and speech development. *Pediatrics*, 1969, 43, 833-839.

Howie, V.M. Acute and recurrent acute otitis media. In B. Jaffe (Ed.), *Hearing loss in children.* Baltimore: University Park Press, 1977.

Jaffe, B. (Ed.) *Hearing loss in children.* Baltimore: University Park Press, 1977.

Kaplan, G.K., Fleshman, J.K., & Bender, T.R., et al. Long term effects of otitis media: a 10-year cohort study of Alaska Eskimo children. *Pediatrics*, 1973, 52, 577-585.

Karchmer, M., Milone, M., & Wolk, S. Educational significance of hearing loss at three severity levels. *Am Ann Deaf* Vol 124, 1979, 97-109.

Katz, J., & Epstein, A. A hypothesis considering non-mechanical aspects of conductive hearing loss. *Acta Otolaryngol*, 1962, 55, 145-150.

Katz, J., & Ullmer, R. Auditory perception in children with learning disabilities. In J. Katz (Ed.), *Handbook of clinical audiology*. Baltimore: Williams & Wilkins, 1972, pp. 540-563.

Katz, J. The effects of conductive hearing loss on auditory function. *ASHA*, 1978, *20*, 879-886.

Kessner, D.M., Snow, C.K., & Singer, J. Assessment of medical care in children. In *Contrasts in health status* (Vol. 30). Washington, D.C.: National Academy of Sciences, Institute of Medicine, 1974.

Lewis, N. Otitis media and linguistic incompetence. *Arch Otolaryngol*, 1976, *102*, 387-390.

Ling, D. Rehabilitation of cases with deafness secondary to otitis media. In A. Glorig & K. Gerwin (Eds.), *Otitis media*. Springfield, Illinois: Charles C. Thomas, 1972, pp. 249-253.

McCandless, G., & Thomas, G. Impedance audiometry as a screening procedure for middle ear disease. *Trans Am Acad Ophthalmol Otolaryngol*, 1974, *78*, 98-102.

Needleman, H. Effects of hearing loss from early otitis media on speech and language development. In B. Jaffe (Ed.), *Hearing loss in children*. Baltimore: University Park Press, 1977.

Northern, J., & Downs, M.P. *Hearing in children* (2nd ed). Baltimore: Williams & Wilkins, 1978.

Quigley, S.P. Some effects of hearing impairment upon school performance. Manuscript prepared for the Division of Special Education Services, Office of the Superintendant of Public Instruction, State of Illinois, 1970.

Rose, S.P., Conneally, P.M., & Nance, W.E. Genetic analysis of childhood deafness. In Bess, F.H. (Ed.), *Childhood Deafness: Causation, Assessment and Management*. New York: Grune & Stratton, 1977.

Schein, J.D., & Delk, M.T. *The deaf population of the United States*. Silver Spring, Maryland: National Association of the Deaf, 1974.

Skinner, M.W. The hearing of speech during language acquisition. *Otolaryngol Clin North Am*, 1978, *11*, 224-232.

Webster, D.B., & Webster, M. Neonatal sound deprivation affects brain stem nuclei. *Arch Otolaryngol*, 1977, *103*, 393-396.

*Ron J. Leavitt*

# 4

# Hearing Aids and Other Amplifying Devices for Hearing-Impaired Children

This chapter describes the basic components of the hearing aid and other amplifying devices, and examines some of the issues associated with successful hearing aid usage. Before purchasing a hearing aid or any other amplifying device, a potential user should seek consultation with local audiology facilities.

## TYPES AND BASIC COMPONENTS OF HEARING AIDS

There are four types of hearing aids currently on the market (see Fig. 4-1) including:

1. behind-the-ear aids, also called postauricular or ear level aids
2. in-the-ear aids
3. eyeglass aids
4. body aids.

Although the four types of hearing aids look different, they share many similarities. For example, all four types require some sort of ear-

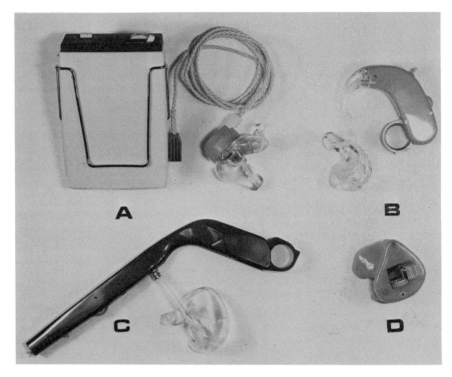

**Figure 4-1.** The four different types of hearing aids include the (A) body aid, (B) behind-the-ear aid, (C) eyeglass aid, and (D) in-the-ear aid.

piece or earmold to hold the aid in the child's ear. Additionally, all four types have a microphone, amplifier, earphone (speaker), and battery.

### The Earmold

The earmold (Fig. 4-2) is a small device made of hard or soft material—usually soft lucite, silicone, or polyvinyl chloride—that fits compactly in the child's ear. When properly fit, the earmold holds the hearing aid (or earphone in the case of a body aid) on the child's ear and directs the amplified sound from the hearing aid into the child's ear canal. If the earmold becomes loose, the amplified sound escapes around the earmold, is reamplified in the hearing aid, and causes the aid to whistle. This whistling is called *acoustic feedback*. When an aid is whistling, it can interfere with the child's reception of sound and is less functional. It is crucial, therefore, to ensure that the child's earmold is always properly fit. With very young children, fitting the earmold

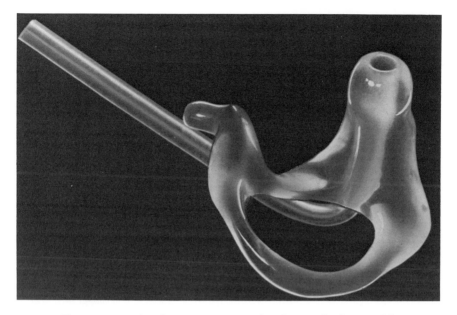

**Figure 4-2.** This figure is an example of a standard earmold.

can be difficult, since the child's ear grows rapidly and requires frequent earmold remakes. One report in the literature (Clark, Watkins, Reese, Allen, Olsen & Berg, 1975) has shown that children under 2 1/2 years of age require a new earmold about every 3 months to prevent acoustic feedback. Between age 2 1/2 to 5 years, the earmold requires replacement about every 6 months, although there is considerable variability from child to child.

## The Hearing Aid Microphone

The hearing aid microphone (Fig.4–3) changes sound into a small electrical signal. This electrical signal then activates the hearing aid's amplifier, which magnifies the signal. The power for this amplification is provided by the hearing aid battery. This amplified electrical signal is then sent to the hearing aid earphone (sometimes called a receiver), where the electrical signal is changed back into sound waves and directed through the earmold to the child's ear canal. Although the location and configuration of the microphone, amplifier, and earphone vary considerably between the four types of aids, the principle of operation is basically the same. In fact, some in-the-ear and behind-the-ear aids use some identical components.

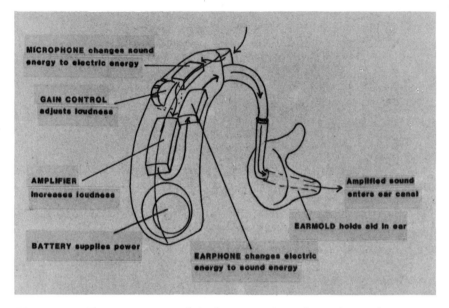

**Figure 4-3.**  The components of the hearing aid are shown here. The arrows trace the path of sound through the aid.

### Volume, or Gain, Control

All four types of hearing aids described above also have a volume, or gain, control (see Fig. 4–3), which allows the hearing aid wearer to adjust the loudness of the incoming speech to a comfortable listening level.

Many hearing aids, regardless of style, incorporate other accessories that may include any or all of the following:

1.  telephone or "T" switch
2.  SSPL control
3.  internal gain control
4.  tone control
5.  compression control.

All of these accessories are included on the ear-level aid in Figure 4–4, and their functions are described below.

### Telephone Switch

The telephone switch allows the hearing aid to respond to magnetic signals such as those produced by a telephone earphone. However, when

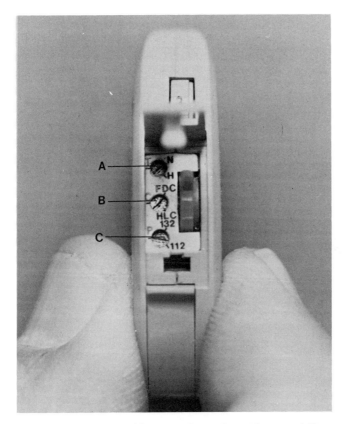

**Figure 4-4.** The variable controls on this aid are as follows (A) tone control, (B) compression control, and (C) the SSPL control.

on "T" setting, the typical aid will not amplify anything else but the phone conversation. Thus, by setting the aid to "T", a child can listen to amplified telephone conversations through the hearing aid and not be bothered by room noises. The "T" setting can also be used to great advantage in classrooms that are equipped with induction loop systems. These are inexpensive amplifying systems that turn the teacher's voice into a magnetic signal that can be picked up by the child's aid when the aid is set on "T". The induction loop will be described in more detail later in this chapter.

## Internal Controls

The SSPL control (formerly known as a maximum power output or MPO control), the internal gain control, the tone control, and the compression control have been referred to collectively as internal controls. These controls allow the audiologist to adjust the hearing aid to the child's specific hearing needs. It is critically important that no one other than a qualified audiologist adjust these controls, since inappropriate settings can decrease the adequacy of the hearing aid fitting that could, in extreme instances, result in further damage to the child's hearing.

## Hearing Aid Procurement

In the not too distant past, potential hearing aid users often obtained a hearing aid by visiting a local hearing aid dealership, listening to a few aids, and selecting the aid that sounded the best and was most acceptable cosmetically. Although sound quality and cosmetic concerns are important, other factors must be considered for the best hearing aid fitting to be achieved. These factors are discussed below.

## Medical Clearance for a Hearing Aid

In 1977, the Food and Drug Administration (FDA) issued the following statement:

> Federal law restricts the sale of hearing aids to those individuals who have obtained a medical evaluation from a licensed physician. Federal law permits a fully informed adult to sign a waiver statement declining the medical evaluation for religious or personal beliefs that preclude consultation with a physician. The exercise of such a waiver is not in your best health interest and its use is strongly discouraged. In addition to a medical evaluation, a child with a hearing loss should be directed to an audiologist for evaluation and rehabilitation, since hearing loss may cause problems in language development, and in education and social growth of a child. An audiologist is qualified by training and experience to assist in the evaluation and rehabilitation of a child with a hearing loss. (p. 9295)

Furthermore, FDA continues:

> A hearing aid dispenser shall not sell a hearing aid unless the prospective user has presented to the hearing aid dispenser a written statement signed by a licensed physician that states that the patient's hearing loss has been medically evaluated and the patient may be considered a candidate for a hearing aid. The medical evaluation must have taken place within the preceeding six months. (p. 9296)

It should be noted that, although the FDA regulations allow for adults 18 years or older to sign the medical waiver, this option is not open to children. This regulation is intended to ensure that no medical condition exists that would be aggravated by hearing aid use. Additionally, some types of conductive hearing loss are medically or surgically treatable (see Chapter 2 for discussion). When treatment is successful, the patient's hearing loss may be totally resolved, obviating the need for a hearing aid.

There are several other reasons why a person who routinely wears a hearing aid should be monitored by a physician at regular intervals:

1.   The hearing aid's earmold may irritate the ear canal and, in very rare cases, result in an allergic skin reaction.

2.   Ear wax (cerumen) build-up may be a problem occasionally, since the earmold plugs the ear, preventing the normal escape route for cerumen.

3.   As Matkin (1981) has pointed out, children with sensorineural hearing loss are still prone to additional conductive loss. If this conductive loss goes unnoticed "inappropriate management may result with respect to hearing aid selection and educational placement."

### Audiological Evaluation

An optimal hearing aid fitting for a child is highly dependent on a complete audiologic and hearing aid evaluation by a trained audiologist. The specific components of a complete audiologic evaluation are beyond the scope of this chapter and will not be discussed here. However, the parent is well advised to obtain audiologic consultation prior to considering the child's hearing aid usage.

### Hearing Aid Selection

Although the specifics of a good hearing aid selection procedure vary among hearing clinics, most audiologists agree that before an aid is purchased, the child should be evaluated with a specific hearing aid, preferably while wearing a custom-made earmold (Burney, 1972; Konkle & Bess, 1974). It is important for parents to realize that, regardless of age, aided testing (testing of a person wearing a hearing aid) is possible and highly desirable. Such testing provides all concerned parties with valuable information. In those instances where the necessary hearing aid fitting information cannot be obtained during the first visit (for example, with children less than 6 months of age), a hearing aid fitting must be viewed as an ongoing process, where the initial fitting is carefully monitored by the parents, audiologist, and teachers and continually refined until optimal aided function is obtained. Fortunately, many hearing aid dispensers offer a 30–day hearing aid trial period for a minimal fee. Thus, if the initial fitting proves unsatisfactory, another aid may be tried without great expense. For this reason, the parents are encouraged to seek hearing aid trial use privileges when selecting the hearing aid dispenser. Alternately, the audiologist may select a recently marketed hearing aid whose internal controls can be adjusted to fit any degree or configuration of hearing loss. In this way, the aid can be "fine tuned" as more audiological information is obtained.

### Parent and Teacher Observation

Parent and teacher observation of the child's aided functioning is an important component of the hearing aid selection procedure. Figure 4–5 provides a formal checklist of the child's aided and unaided auditory behavior that can be useful when assessing the adequacy of a hearing aid fitting. It is anticipated generally that the greater the child's hearing loss, the fewer auditory behaviors are typically noted. For example, children with profound fragmented hearing losses (see Chapter 2) who have good hearing aid fittings will show typically less responsiveness to sound than their aided peers who have mild to moderate losses.

### Artificial Ear Measures

In addition to the aided measures that are obtained while the child is wearing the aid (which are frequently referred to as "real ear" aided measures), electronic measurements of the amplifying characteristics of the aid should also be made. These measurements are obtained by equipment called *electroacoustic analyzers*. Since the measurements are made without the child wearing the aid, the analyzer must utilize a metal cavity to simulate some of the characteristics of the human ear (hence, the term "artificial ear" measures). These "artificial ear" measures permit a standardized comparison of the child's aid to the ideal specifications provided by the manufacturer. In this way, it is possible to ascertain the aid's proper functioning before trying it on the client. It is important to note that these "artificial ear" measures cannot substitute for "real ear" aided measures (those obtained while the child wears the aid). Instead, the artificial ear measures supplement the real ear measures and may identify subtle problems exhibited by the aid, per se, not readily apparent during real ear aided testing (Lybarger, 1975; Studebaker, Cox, & Wark, 1978; Studebaker & Zachman, 1970; van Eysbergen & Groen, 1959).

### Binaural Hearing Aid Usage

Another issue that must be decided when selecting amplification is whether the child is going to wear one (monaural) or two (binaural)

**Figure 4-5.** The check list of listening behavior includes environmental sounds, general communication, and speech sounds.

Please Note: Because children with hearing loss learn to rely on their vision, it is important that when answering the following questions you make sure the child cannot see you. In other words, only check "yes" on the questionnaire when you are sure the child heard something and had no chance of getting any visual clues.

## ENVIRONMENTAL SOUNDS

CHECK ONE

When wearing aid
Yes     No
When not wearing aid
Yes     N0

1. Does the child look up when an airplane is passing over?

When wearing aid
Yes     No
When not wearing aid
Yes     No

2. Does the child startle when something is dropped on the floor and makes a loud nosie?

When wearing aid
Yes     No
When not wearing aid
Yes     No

3. Does the child startle to sounds at home, such as a door slamming?

When wearing aid
Yes     No
When not wearing aid
Yes     No

4. Does the child turn to look in the direction of a door that has slammed rather than startle?

When wearing aid
Yes     No
When not wearing aid
Yes     No

5. Does the child become alert or look out the window when a noisy truck, car, or motorcycle passes by?

When wearing aid
Yes     No
When not wearing aid
Yes     No

6. Does the child alert or look out the window when a dog is barking outside?

When wearing aid
Yes     No
When not wearing aid
Yes     No

7. Does the child watch television with the volume set at a level that is too loud for you?

When wearing aid
Yes     No
When not wearing aid
Yes     No

8. Does the child show an interest in toys that make noise? If Yes, Please describe: _____
_____
_____
_____

_____
_____
_____
_____
_____
_____
_____
_____

When wearing aid
Yes    No

9. Does the child hear a car driving up in the driveway?

## GENERAL COMMUNICATION

When wearing aid
Yes    No
When not wearing aid
Yes    No

1. When you stand behind the child and call his/her name in a loud voice, does he/she alert or turn to look at you?

When wearing aid
Yes    No
When not wearing aid
Yes    No

2. Does the child come to you when you call him from another room?

When wearing aid
Yes    No
When not wearing aid
Yes    No

3. Will the child try to imitate something that is said on the television?

When wearing aid
Yes    No
When not wearing aid

4. Does the child try to imitate things that you have said?

## SPEECH SOUNDS

When wearing aid
Yes    No
When not wearing aid
Yes    No

1. Can the child imitate you if you cover your mouth, stand in front of him, and say "buh, buh, buh" in a normal voice?

When wearing aid
Yes    No
When not wearing aid
Yes    No

2. Can the child imitate you when you cover your mouth, stand in front of him, and say "oh, oh, oh" in a normal voice?

When wearing aid
Yes    No
When not wearing aid
Yes    No

3. Can the child imitate you when you cover your mouth, stand in front of him, and say "ah, ah, ah" in a normal voice?

48

| When wearing aid | 4. | Can the child imitate you when you cover |
|---|---|---|
| Yes     No | | your mouth, stand in front of him, and say |
| When not wearing aid | | "ee, ee, ee" in a normal voice? |
| Yes     No | | |

| When wearing aid | 5. | Can the child imitate you when you cover |
|---|---|---|
| Yes     No | | your mouth, stand in front of him, and say |
| When not wearing aid | | "sh, sh, sh" in a normal voice? |
| Yes     No | | |

| When wearing aid | 6. | Can the child imitate you when you stand |
|---|---|---|
| Yes     No | | in front of him, cover your mouth, and say |
| When not wearing aid | | "s, s, s" in a normal voice? |
| Yes     No | | |

aids. Much disagreement exists in this area among audiologists. However, Mark Ross, a noted audiologist, reviewed a number of well-controlled studies (Ross, 1977) and concluded that the majority of these studies showed a superiority for binaural hearing aid usage. It is still true, however, that some children are not good binaural hearing aid candidates, which again underscores the importance of consultation with an audiologist.

## HEARING AID USAGE

Once adequate real and artificial ear measurements have been obtained, considerable follow up is necessary before successful hearing aid usage is achieved. Issues related to this important area are noted below.

### Parental Expectation

The first issue associated with successful hearing aid usage is realistic parental expectation. The parents must realize that the hearing aid does not restore hearing to normal. This is especially true for children with profound bilateral sensorineural hearing losses. As mentioned in Chapters 1 and 2, when a child has a sensorineural hearing impairment, there is a loss of both loudness and clarity for speech. Since the hearing aid provides primarily an increase in speech loudness, the hearing-impaired child will still experience some distortion when listening to speech through the aid. The greater the child's sensorineural hearing loss, the greater this distortion will be. Thus, the child must be trained to make maximum use of the speech that is amplified by the aid.

## Strategies for Facilitating Hearing Aid Usage

Those working with hearing-impaired children will benefit from some basic strategies that will help the child hear better through the hearing aid. Some of these strategies are described below.

THE CHILD SHOULD BE AS CLOSE AS POSSIBLE TO THE SPEAKER.    Both in individual and audience-type listening conditions, the child should be as close as possible to those who are speaking. This will give the child the best opportunity to use his or her residual hearing. Finally, the common practice of talking at home with the parent in one room and the child in another should be modified to accommodate the child.

HEARING AID SHOULD BE DIRECTED TOWARD THE SPEAKER.    Children who wear one hearing aid should learn to direct the aid toward the speaker. When several people are talking, they should learn to structure their position in the room so they can orient the hearing aid toward the speaker of greatest interest.

ENVIRONMENTAL NOISE SOURCES SHOULD BE REDUCED AS MUCH AS POSSIBLE.    Hearing-impaired persons should stay away from common noise sources such as fans, vents, motors, or open windows. When possible, they should orient themselves so that their hearing aid is toward the speaker and the unaided ear toward major noise sources in the room. To best serve the hearing-impaired child, parents may wish to turn off background sounds such as radio or television. Windows admitting traffic noise or other sounds should be closed.

THE CHILD SHOULD WATCH FACES.    The child should be encouraged to keep line of sight with the speaker and to arrange for adequate light on the speaker's face. Backlighting conditions should be avoided, since it makes it more difficult to watch the speaker's face.

PEOPLE SHOULD BE TOLD ABOUT THE CHILD'S HEARING LOSS.    If others know about the loss, they may be asked to speak slowly and distinctly. Knowledge of the loss will help others to appreciate why the hard-of-hearing child does not always respond appropriately (Hodgson, 1981).

## The Child's Acceptance of an Aid

At times, a child may not readily accept a hearing aid. For this reason, Downs (1967) has recommended a gradually progressive schedule of hearing aid usage for the child. This schedule allows the child to gradually adjust to the hearing aid:

FIRST WEEK.  The aid should be put on for a short time (5 minutes or so) several times each day. The parent should be firm, and if the child should protest actively, the parent should persist and restrain the child if necessary. After the child accepts the aid, the procedure should be repeated with the gain turned to a low level in a quiet room. The parent can talk to the child and play favorite games.

SECOND WEEK.  The aided periods should be expanded to 15 minutes or so, several times each day, with the volume control set a little higher. The sounds made by various objects, such as the doorbell, the refrigerator, and other things around the house should be emphasized.

THIRD WEEK.  Hearing aid use can be expanded to 30-minute periods several times daily. The child should wear the aid while a parent does household tasks, pointing out the relationship between movements and the sounds they make.

FOURTH WEEK.  Aided periods can be expanded to 45 minutes several times each day. The hearing aid's volume control should almost be set to the recommended level.

FIFTH WEEK.  Aided periods should be expanded to 1 hour in duration.

SIXTH WEEK AND AFTERWARDS.  Use of the aid should be continued until, by the second month, the child is using the hearing aid full time. Exceptions may consist of (1) brief unamplified "rest periods," (2) nap time, and (3) rough play outdoors.

Occasionally, at about 12 years of age or so, a hearing aid wearer who has previously accepted the hearing aid may suddenly reject it. Sometimes this occurs because the child is becoming more aware of personal appearance and more concerned about appearing different than his or her hearing peers. Some important considerations about this problem in adolescence are described below (adapted from Hodgson, 1981):

1.  A parent should not say "nonsense" or belittle the problem. These feelings should be acknowledged as important, and they should receive attention.
2.  "Prevention is better than cure." A good training program will lead to effective use and less tendency to reject the aid (again underscoring the importance of aural habilitation).
3.  A child should be helped to understand that his or her behavior is less different with the aid than it is without it.

4. An adult should try to prevent the child from being teased.
5. If needed, a child's cosmetic appearances can be improved. For example, it is often possible to change from a body aid to a behind-the-ear aid, or to change the child's hairstyle.
6. Parental attitudes and parent/child relationships are important, and the parent should realize that adolescents need a lot of support (p. 244).

## Controlling Environmental Noise

In addition to a gradually progressive program of hearing aid usage, the child with a hearing aid should also be provided with a quiet listening environment when first starting to use the aid. After the child becomes more accustomed to hearing soft sounds through the hearing aid, the noise level in the environment can be increased gradually.

Hodgson (1981) has outlined a gradually progressive set of listening situations, beginning with hearing aid use in a quiet home living room listening to one person talking, and then progressing to somewhat more acoustically varied environments, such as home-listening situations where one person is talking with a minimum of background noise like the television or one other family member. Such a gradual introduction of background noise will reduce the possibility that the child may be frightened by loud unfamiliar noises during the early stages of hearing aid use. The interested reader is referred to the Hodgson publication for further discussion.

## Control of Classroom Noise

It is also important that the hearing-impaired child be provided an appropriately quiet classroom environment. Research has shown that a child with a hearing loss has great difficulty understanding normal conversation in even moderately noisy environments (Finitzo-Heiber & Tillman, 1978; Gengel, 1971; Tillman, Carhart & Olsen, 1970). There are several reasons for this difficulty with hearing in a noisy setting:

1. The child's aid also amplifies room noise, such as the heater and air conditioner, as well as the signal of interest (such as the teacher's voice). This noise tends to mask out the teacher's voice, especially when the child is seated near the source of noise and away from the teacher. Clearly, such a seating arrangement is to be avoided since every hearing-impaired child will tend to function less efficiently in this situation.

2. Research has shown that people who possess sensorineural losses have greater difficulty understanding speech even in relatively low noise levels with or without an aid (Gengel, 1971).

## Control of Echoes (Reverberation) in the Classroom

In addition to problems hearing in a noisy setting, hearing-impaired children also have difficulty hearing speech when the speech signal is reflected off hard surfaces such as walls, uncarpeted floors, windows, and blackboards. Some research has even suggested that the combined effect of room noise and a highly echoic room is even more debilitating than would be predicted by assessing the contribution of each variable separately (Finitzo-Hieber & Tillman, 1978; Gelfand & Hochberg, 1976; Nabelek & Pickett, 1974 a,b).

Obviously, it is important to try to reduce both reverberation and noise in the hearing-impaired child's environment by proper acoustic treatment of classrooms and all learning environments. Such acoustic treatment can often be attained rather inexpensively by proper use of curtains, rugs, and acoustic tile. For a more detailed discussion of this issue, the interested reader is referred to Beranek (1954).

## Hearing Aid Care

The parents and the child must learn how to adjust the aid's volume control, replace the hearing aid batteries, use the telephone switch, place the earmold in the child's ear, and trouble-shoot the hearing aid. The parents must be certain that the audiologist provides a detailed explanation of the items listed above. A hearing aid trouble-shooting guide is provided later in this chapter, and some general rules for hearing aid care are listed below.

1. Do not expose the aid unnecessarily to dust, dirt, heat, humidity, or other moisture. Do not leave it in a hot place, such as near a radiator or in front of a window where the sun shines directly on it. Remove the aid before applying hair spray.
2. Do not drop the aid.
3. Remove the batteries if the aid is to be unused for some time.
4. Keep the earmold clean. Gently detach the earmold and tubing from the hearing aid. Wash in soapy water, cleaning all earwax from the earmold. Rinse thoroughly. Dry carefully, being sure all water is removed from tube and sound bore. Reattach the earmold tubing to the earhook. Do not wash all in-the-ear aids.

5.  Keep aids out of reach of children and pets. Have a safe place des-
    ignated to put the aid when not worn. Do not use any fluids in an
    attempt to clean or repair the aid. Reserve all repairs other than the
    simple trouble-shooting procedures discussed in this chapter for
    qualified service people.
6.  Have the performance of the aid checked at each audiologic eval-
    uation (adapted from Hodgson, 1981).

## HEARING AID FOLLOW-UP

### Aural Habilitation

Formal training with the hearing aid is necessary so that residual
hearing is used to its utmost. This training is currently termed *aural
habilitation*. Aural habilitation is discussed in more detail in Chapters
6, 8, and 9, so it will not receive detailed coverage here. Such training
is critical to the optimal functioning of the hearing-impaired child.

### Audiological and Hearing Aid Re-evaluations

Audiological and hearing aid re-evaluation should be scheduled
at regular intervals. Matkin (1981) recommends the following re-evaluation schedule:

1.  During the first year of hearing aid usage, audiological and hearing
    aid evaluations should be scheduled at least every 3 months (or
    sooner if unexpected problems are encountered with the child's
    hearing aid or hearing).
2.  For preschool children who have used a hearing aid at least 1 year,
    re-evaluations should be scheduled every 6 months.
3.  For school-age children who have worn a hearing aid for at least
    one year, re-evaluations should be scheduled annually.

This schedule seems appropriate for several reasons. For example,
school-age children need to have their earmolds replaced frequently,
since their ears grow rapidly, resulting in loose-fitting earmolds and
acoustic feedback.

Another reason for frequent audiological follow-up is to monitor
possible changes in the child's hearing sensitivity. As Matkin (1981)
has pointed out, several genetic and viral sensorineural losses are believed to be progressive. Thus, frequent hearing evaluation is essential
so that proper medical attention, educational management, and hearing
aid adjustments can be assured. Furthermore, as mentioned previously,

children who possess nonprogressive sensorineural hearing losses may also experience occasional middle ear problems, which can result in temporary hearing deterioration that is greater than experienced with the sensorineural hearing loss alone.

These children must also be followed at regular intervals throughout the school years. These regular audiological visits give the audiologist an opportunity to provide parental support, reduce the parent's fears, and answer questions that may not have occurred to parents during the initial evaluation. Regular audiological and hearing aid evaluations during the preschool and school-age years also provide an opportunity for the audiologist to "fine tune" the hearing aid fitting. This is frequently necessary with difficult-to-test children, where somewhat limited audiological information may have been obtained during early visits.

Regular audiologic evaluation is also necessary to monitor the effect the hearing aid has on the child's hearing. In most cases the hearing aid will not have any detrimental effect on the child's hearing. However, in a small number of children, the hearing aid has been shown to damage hearing. This subject has received detailed coverage elsewhere (Rintelmann & Bess, 1977). To summarize their findings, the following generalizations seem warranted:

1.  Damage to hearing due to overamplification can occur from hearing aid usage in a small number of children (Naunton, 1957; Kinney, 1961; Sataloff, 1961.; Macrae & Farrant, 1965; Barr & Wedenberg, 1965; Ross & Truex, 1965; Ross & Lerman, 1967; Bellefleur & Van Dyke, 1968; Kasten & Braulin, 1970; Madell & Asp, 1970; Roberts, 1970; Jerger & Lewis, 1975).
2.  This deterioration in hearing is often temporary, and hearing often returns to pre-aided levels when the hearing aid is removed from the child's ear, or when the hearing aid is alternated between ears (Harford & Markle, 1955; Kasten & Braulin, 1970; Macrae, 1968; Statloff, 1961).
3.  High power hearing aids present a greater risk to the child's hearing than mild and moderate power instruments (Barr & Wedenberg, 1965; Bellefleur & Van Dyke, 1968; Farrant, 1965; Jerger & Lewis, 1975; Kasten & Braulin, 1970; Kinney, 1961; Konkle & Rintelmann, 1976; Macrae, 1968; Macrae & Farrant, 1965; Madell & Asp, 1970; Naunton, 1957; Roberts, 1970; Ross & Lerman, 1967; Ross & Truex, 1965; Sataloff, 1961). Since children with severe and profound losses require hearing aids with more power than children with mild to moderate losses, it is important to frequently monitor the child's hearing.

4.  The *maximum power output* (MPO) of the aid, also called *saturation sound pressure level* (SSPL), must be set at an appropriate level. The audiologist can achieve this by proper setting of the aid's internal controls. There is some evidence that the likelihood of hearing loss due to overamplification from hearing aid use can be reduced if the SSPL is set at an appropriate level. In fact, the FDA (1977) has ruled that any hearing aid that has an SSPL exceeding 132dB shall be labeled with a warning that "use of such an instrument may have deleterious effects on hearing." However, some clinical evidence suggests that, for children, even 130dB may be too high a level (Macrae & Farrant, 1965; Rintelmann, 1975; Ross & Lerman, 1967). From a review of the literature, it can be suggested, with much support, that a child whose aid exceeds 120dB SSPL should be monitored audiologically very closely. Additionally, any child who wears a hearing aid should be discouraged from using that aid in high noise levels such as when in automotive, metal, or wood shops; when listening to loud music, such as a live concert; or when attending motorboat, water-skiing, or drag races, since these high noise levels can result rapidly in further hearing damage. If a child is going to be near such high levels of noise, the hearing aid should not be worn, and effective hearing protection (preferably earmuffs) must be utilized.

5.  If the result of the routine hearing test suggests that the hearing aid is possibly causing further deterioration of the child's hearing, binaural hearing aid use should be discouraged; if both ears can be aided, one hearing aid should be alternated between the two ears (Jerger & Lewis, 1975).

In summary, hearing damage from hearing aid use does occur in children. But with careful audiological monitoring and proper setting of the aid's power output, the problem can be minimized. Without the hearing aid, the hearing-impaired child will certainly experience speech and language problems. Thus, the parent should not interpret the findings reported above as discouraging hearing aid usage. Instead, this information provides a strong argument for regular hearing tests and appropriate hearing aid fittings, again underscoring the importance of careful medical monitoring and regular consultation with a qualified audiologist.

## HEARING AID TROUBLE-SHOOTING

Although the development of the electret microphone and the integrated circuit have made the hearing aid a durable instrument, hearing aid malfunction continues to be a considerable problem (Gaeth &

**Figure 4-6.** If the hearing aid malfunctions, here are a few simple troubleshooting suggestions. Try the following if these symptoms occur:

1. *No sound from the aid.* If the aid has an off, on, or telephone switch, be sure the switch is set to "on" or "microphone" position. The battery may be dead. Check the battery voltage or try a new battery. The battery may be in backwards. Be sure that the + sign on the battery is matched with + sign on the battery compartment. The battery may be the wrong size. Check to be sure that the number on the back of the battery is the correct one for the aid. Corrrosion on the battery may prevent the aid from working. Gently remove the corrosion with a sharpened pencil eraser. Check the earmold. The sound channel may be plugged with wax. With the aid on the ear, have someone look at the tubing. It may be twisted and closed, blocking sound. If these checks do not sovle the problem, the aid should be taken in for repair.

2. *Intermittent sound.* The aid is sometimes on, sometimes off. On bodyworn aids, a broken cord or loose connection may be the problem. First, twist the cord and then the connections back and forth at either end. If the aid goes on and off, the cord should be replaced or taken in for repair.

3. *Loudness does not change smoothly* as the volume control is turned up—either the aid is always loud or sound comes on suddenly when the volume control reaches a certain point. The volume control is defective and requires repair or replacement. See the hearing aid dispenser.

4. *Sound from the aid is weak.* The battery may be weak. Check the battery voltage or compare the aid's peformance with a new battery. Check the earmold. The sound channel may be partially obscured by wax. With the aid on the ear, have someone look at the sound tubing. The tubing may be "kinked" and partially closed, reducing sound volume.

5. *The aid is noisy,* producing sounds other than those received by the hearing aid microphone. Move the volume control and the off-on switch back and forth several times. Doing so may remove tiny dirt particles that interfere with operation.

6. *The quality is not natural*—sounds are distorted. The battery may be weak. Try a new battery. If there is a tone control, be sure it is set in its customary position. If these things do not help, the aid probably requires repair.

7. *The aid squeals* when turned to a volume control setting less than that needed for good amplification. Be sure the earmold is seated properly and that it fits well. If not, sound leaking from the earmold will cause squealing. The same is true of sound leaking from the tubing or the earhook. If the earmold tubing or earhook are cracked, they must be replaced. See the hearing aid dispenser.

Lounsbury, 1966). Figure 4–6 presents a hearing aid trouble-shooting check list. This check list will frequently identify the source of the problem and suggest a simple and inexpensive solution. At other times, however, considerable repair may be necessary. When repair is required, the hearing aid should be returned to the hearing aid dispenser for shipment to the manufacturer. Since few hearing aid dealers do their own repair work, the child may be without a hearing aid for as long as several weeks. Thus, before choosing a hearing aid dispenser, the possibility of obtaining loaner aids should be ascertained.

## AUDITORY TRAINERS

As mentioned earlier in this chapter, when the child is wearing an aid in a classroom situation, background noise and reflected sound are amplified as well as the teacher's voice. In some circumstances, the classroom noise may even be amplified more than the teacher's voice if the child is closer to the source of the noise (classmates, heating and air conditioning ducts, and moving chairs). To alleviate some of this problem, auditory trainers may be a most appropriate choice in the classroom environment. Although there are different types of auditory trainers, they are similar in that they bring the voice of the teacher closer to the hearing-impaired child's ear, and they are not as susceptible to environmental noise. Figure 4–7 shows a number of auditory trainers that can be classified as (A) hard wire systems, (B) induction loops, (C) radio frequency systems (FM or AM), and (D) infrared systems. Each system is discussed separately below.

### Hard Wire Systems

The hard wire system (see Fig. 4–7A) is the oldest of the auditory training systems. This system requires nothing more than a microphone, an amplifier with microphone input, and a set of earphones. In other words, this system has the same components as an ordinary hearing aid. The only major difference is that it is larger, and the microphone is worn by the teacher. Because of its simplicity, the hard wire system is relatively inexpensive.

The major disadvantage of the hard wire system is that it is quite cumbersome, since wires must run from the microphone to the amplifier, and from the amplifier to the earphones. Thus, both teacher and student have limited movement, making the system of little value for field trips, school assemblies, and other activities outside the classroom.

## Induction Loop System

The student mobility can be enhanced, somewhat, by use of a device called an induction loop (review Fig. 4–7A). The induction loop can be used only by children who have hearing aids that incorporate a telephone or "T" switch. The induction loop is nothing more than a length of wire that generates a magnetic signal that is picked up by the child's aid set to its telephone switch. Because an induction loop can typically be added to a hard wired system at a low cost, it can be used in a variety of settings. It is highly recommended, however, that the child's telephone setting on his or her aid is evaluated before such use, since research has shown that hearing aids frequently do not function as well when set to the "T" setting (Matkin & Olsen, 1970, a,b).

With a good "T" switch (telephone circuit) on the aid, and an appropriately constructed induction loop system, a good signal can be provided to the child for a low cost at home, school, church, and theater settings. Additionally, a small portable induction loop can be built to optimize the child's speech understanding for television, radio, and tape recorders for under five dollars at present costs. The material needed to construct such a system can be obtained by writing the author of this chapter. This miniature loop is shown connected to an ordinary portable radio in Figure 4–7B.

## Radio Frequency Systems

This group of auditory trainers operates like a minature radio broadcasting station. As can be seen in Figure 4–7C, the teacher wears the microphone that has an AM or FM radio transmitter built into it. The transmitter then broadcasts to a receiving device that is worn by the hearing-impaired child. This receiving device is just like a transistor radio. The only major difference is that this receiver is permanently set to a single station usually. In fact, in some public meeting places, ordinary transistor radios can be used, permitting anyone that has a radio to benefit from the amplification. However, for a hearing-impaired child in a classroom situation, the ordinary transistor radio system is not recommended.

Because the radio frequency systems incorporate relatively sophisticated radio transmitters, they are more expensive than all other systems. However, when fit appropriately for the child, an excellent high fidelity speech signal can be sent to the child, and great mobility is possible. Thus, the child can receive the benefits of a clear speech signal in the classroom, on a field trip, at home, at theaters and churches, or in any other listening situation. Additionally, some of these units often have what is called an "auxiliary input" that allows the transmitter

A

B

C

D

**Figure 4-7.A** The hard wire system with earphones or induction loop is shown. The microphone is in front; the amplifier with its tone and volume controls is in the center of the picture; the induction loop is the coil of wire surrounding the amplifier; and the earphones are to the right of the amplifier.

**Figure 4-7B.** This figure shows the miniature neck-work induction loop plugged into an ordinary portable radio.

**Figure 4-7C.** In this FM radio frequency system, the microphone and FM transmitter are hand-held, and the receiver is worn on the belt.

**Figure 4-7D.** The infrared system is shown, in which the microphone and transmitter are in the author's hand, and the infrared receiver is clipped to the belt.

61

to be plugged directly into a television, radio, tape recorder, or film projector so that the same high quality signal can be sent to the child without picking up any background noise.

Radio frequency systems can work with the portable induction loop described previously. In this way, the child can use either an earphone that comes with the radio frequency receiver unit, or listen through his or her own hearing aid set on the telephone switch.

Ross (1982) has noted that the FM type auditory trainer gives a stronger and clearer signal than the AM system, especially when other electrical devices are operating near the auditory trainer. For this reason, if a choice is available between AM and FM systems, the FM system seems preferable at present.

### Infrared Systems

Recently infrared light auditory training systems have been developed. These systems are similar to the radio frequency systems in that a microphone with a built-in transmitter is worn by the teacher, and the hearing-impaired child wears a receiver (See Fig. 4–7D). Instead of transmission of radio signals, however, the infrared system transmits infrared light to the receiver. This receiver then changes the light signal back into an acoustic signal. At present, the infrared system is slightly less expensive than most of the radio frequency systems. However, these infrared systems cannot function in sunlight or near bright incandescent lights. Additionally, black velvet curtains absorb the light waves (Ross, 1982), and when a small infrared transmitter is used, the children must be restricted in their movement since blockage of the transmitter's light results in the signal not being received. Thus, for children in an educational setting, the infrared system has several limitations.

### OTHER ACCESSORIES FOR THE HEARING IMPAIRED

In addition to hearing aids, induction loops, and auditory trainers, a number of other accessories are available for hearing-impaired children and adults. These devices are listed in Appendix 4–1, along with the suppliers' addresses. Unfortunately, some distributors, such as Hal Hen, do not sell direct to the public; parents should consult with the company to find a local supplier. Due to space constraints, these devices cannot be described in detail. Again, the parent or teacher should consult with a knowledgeable audiologist or sales representative to get more detailed information.

## CONCLUSION

In summary, all hearing aids, regardless of style, can be viewed as miniature public address systems that contain a microphone, amplifier, and earphone. These components are also present in the various types of auditory trainers that may incorporate radio frequency or infrared light transmitters and receivers. Both hearing aids and auditory trainers can make sounds louder and, by virtue of increased loudness and selective amplification of frequencies, a little clearer. When sensorineural hearing loss exists, however, some distortion will still be present in the speech signal. In general, the greater the sensorineural hearing loss, the greater distortion built into the child's ear. Thus, it is important for parents, family members, and all concerned parties to realize that, although a hearing aid can be of significant benefit, the hearing aid does not "cure" a hearing loss. The auditory trainer can greatly enhance the child's hearing in classrooms and other noisy situations; however, even the best auditory trainers cannot offer perfect word understanding.

## REFERENCES

Barr, B., & Wedenberg, E. Prognosis of perceptive hearing loss in children with respect to genesis and use of hearing aid. *Acta Otolaryngology*, 1965, *59*, 462-474.

Bellefleur, P.A., & Van Dyke, R.C. The effects of high gain amplification on children in a residential school for the deaf. *Speech Hearing Research*, 1968, *11*, 343-347.

Beranek, L. *Acoustics*. New York: McGraw-Hill Company, 1954.

Burney, P. A survey of hearing aid evaluation procedures. *ASHA*, 1972, *14*, 439-444.

Clark, T., Watkins, S., Reese, R., Allen, A., Olsen, S., & Berg, F. *Programming for hearing impaired infants through amplification and home intervention*. Unpublished paper, Utah State University, Logan, Utah, 1975.

Downs. M., The establishment of hearing aid use: A program for parents. *Maico Audiological Library Series*, 4, report 5, 1967.

Finitzo-Hieber, T., & Tillman, T.W. Room acoustic effects on monosyllabic word discrimination ability for normal and hearing-impaired children. *J. Speech Hearing Research*, 1978, *21*, 440-448.

Food and Drug Administration. Hearing aid devices—professional and patient labeling and conditions for sale. *Federal Register*, February 15, 1977, *42*, 9268-9296.

Gaeth, J., & Lounsbury E. Hearing aids for children in elementary schools. *J. Speech and Hearing Disorders*, 1966, *31*, 283-289.

Gelfand, S.A., & Hochberg, I. Binaural and monaural speech discrimination under reverberation. *Audiology*, 1976, *15*, 72-84.

Gengel, E.W. Acceptable speech-to-noise ratios for aided speech discrimination by the hearing impaired. *J. Auditory Research*, 1971, *11*, 219-222.

Harford, E.R., & Markle, D.M. The atypical effect of a hearing aid on one patient with congenital deafness. *Laryngoscope*, 1955, *65*, 970-972.

Hodgson, W.R. Learning hearing aid use. In W. Hodgson & P. Skinner (Eds.), *Hearing aid assessment and use in audiologic habilitation* (2nd ed.). Baltimore: University Park Press, 1981, chapter 11.

Jerger, J.F., & Lewis N. Binaural hearing aids: are they dangerous for hearing? Arch. Oto-laryngology, 1975, 101, 480-483.

Kasten, R.N., & Braulin, R.J. Traumatic hearing aid usage: a case study. Paper presentation at the American Speech and Hearing Association, New York, 1970.

Kinney, C.E. The further destruction of partially deafened children's hearing by the use of powerful hearing aids. Ann. Otolaryngology, 1961, 70, 828-835.

Konkle, D., & Bess, F. Custom-made versus stock earmolds in hearing aid evaluations. Arch. Otolaryngology, 1974, 99, 140-144.

Konkle, D.F. & Rintelmann, W.F. Temporary threshold shift in children after hearing aid use. Unpublished study, University of Pennsylvania, School of Medicine, Philadelphia, 1976.

Lybarger, S. Comparison of earmold characteristics measured on the 2-cc coupler, the Zwislocki coupler, and real ears. Scand. Audiology Supplement, 1975, 5, 65-85.

Macrae, J.H. TTS and recovery from TTS after use of powerful hearing aids. J.Acoust. Society of America, 1968, 43, 1445-1446.

Macrae, J.H., Farrant, J.H. The effect of hearing aid use on the residual hearing of children with sensorineural deafness, Ann. Otol., 74, 409-419, 1965.

Madell, J.R., & Asp, C.W. The effects of hearing aid amplification on pure tone thresholds of preschool deaf children. Paper presentation at the American Speech and Hearing Association Convention, New York, 1970.

Matkin, N.D. Hearing aids for children. In W.R. Hodgson & P. Skinner (Eds.), Hearing aid assessment and use in audiologic habilitation (2nd ed.). Baltimore: University Park Press, 1981, p. 173.

Matkin, N., & Olsen, W. Response of hearing aids with induction loop amplification system. Am. Ann. Deaf. 115, 73-78 (1970a).

Matkin, N., & Olsen, W. Induction loop amplification systems: classroom performance. ASHA, 12, 239-244 (1970b).

Nabelek, A.K., & Pickett, J.M. Reception of consonants in a classroom as affected by monaural and binaural listening, noise, reverberation, and hearing aids. J. Acoust. Society of America, 1974, 56, 628-639.

Nabelek, A.K., & Pickett, J.M. Monaural and binaural speech perception through hearing aids under noise and reverberation with normal and hearing-impaired listeners. J. Speech Hear. Res., 17, 724-739 (1974b).

Naunton, R.F. The effect of hearing aid use upon the user's residual hearing. Laryngoscope, 1957, 67, 569-576.

Rintelmann, W.R. The potential hazard to hearing from radio frequency auditory training units. Unpublished study, Michigan State University, East Lansing, 1975.

Rintelmann, W.R. & Bess, F.H. High level amplification and potential hearing loss in children. In Bess, F.H. (Ed.), Childhood deafness. New York: Grune and Stratton, 1977.

Roberts, C. Can hearing aids damage hearing? Acta Otolaryngology, 1970, 69, 123-125.

Ross, M. Binaural versus monaural hearing aid amplification for hearing impaired individuals. In Bess, F.H. (Ed.) Childhood deafness. New York: Grune and Stratton, 1977, 235-250.

Ross, M. Communication access for the hearing impaired. Hearing Instruments, 1982, 33, 7-9.

Ross, M., & Lerman, J. Hearing aid usage and its effect upon residual hearing. Arch. Otolaryngology, 1967, 86, 639-644.

Ross, M. & Truex, E.H. Protecting residual hearing in hearing aid users. Arch. Otolaryngology, 82, 1965, 615-617.

Sataloff, J. Pitfalls in routine hearing testing. Arch. Otolaryngology, 1961, 73, 409-419.

Studebaker, G., & Zachman, T. Investigation of the acoustics of earmold vents. J. Acoust. Society of America, 1970, 47, 1107-1115.

Studebaker, G., Cox, R., & Wark, D. Earmold modification effect measured by coupler, threshold and probe techniques. *Audiology*, 1978, *17*, 173-186.

Tillman, T., Carhart, R., & Olsen, W. Hearing aid efficiency in a competing speech situation. *J. Speech Hearing Research*, 1970, *13*, 789-811.

van Eysbergen, H., & Groen, J. The 2-ml coupler and the high frequency performance of hearing aids. *Acustica*, 1959, *9*, 381-386.

# Appendix 4-1. Accessories and their Suppliers for the Hearing Impaired

## TELEVISION AMPLIFIER AND HEARING AID BACK–UP

Radio Shack

Archer 200 milliwatt amplifier
Catalog number 277-1008A

Realistic tie clip Mike
Catalogue number 33-1058

High fidelity earphone

## SPEAKING TUBE (EAR TRUMPET)

HAL HEN COMPANY
36-14 Eleventh Street
Long Island City, NY 11106
Telephone: 212/392-6020

Catalogue number: 770, Speaking Tube

Mid Audio Inc.
120 East Ogden
Hinsdale, IL 60521
Telephone: 1-800-323-6556, Ext. R59

Catalogue number: 211

## BATTERY TESTERS

HAL HEN COMPANY

Catalogue number: 2316, Mini Lite Tester

Radio Shack

Catalogue number: 22-027, Micronta Multi Tester

## TELEPHONE AMPLIFIERS

HAL HEN COMPANY

Catalogue number: 978, Nuvox Telephone Amplifier

OR

Catalogue number: 2222, Nuvox Telephone Coupler
(Cannot be used without a hearing aid that has a telecoil switch)

Mid Audio Inc.

Catalogue numbers: 251, 301, 311, 321, 331, and 334
(order catalogue for complete description)

## PILLOW VIBRATING ALARM CLOCKS

HAL HEN COMPANY

Catalogue number: 2332, Electro Alarm Clock Kit

OR

Catalogue number: 2318, Portable Wake Alarm Kit

Mid Audio Inc.

Catalogue numbers: 105, 541, 551, 601, 611, 621, and 631 (see catalogue
for details)

## LAMPS THAT LIGHT WHEN PHONE OR DOORBELL SOUNDS

HAL HEN COMPANY

Catalogue number: 2139 Sound Lamp with one Microphone

OR

Catalogue number: 2335, Super Sound Lamp with 2 microphones

Mid Audio Inc.

Catalogue numbers: 641, 651, 661, and 709 (see catalogue for details)

## VERY LOUD DOORBELLS AND STROBE LIGHT DOORBELLS

HAL HEN COMPANY

Catalogue number: 2419, High Intensity Doorbell

Mid Audio Inc.

Catalogue numbers: 354, 355, 411, 421, 431, and 441 (see catalogue for
details)

## HEARING AID STETHOSCOPES

These allow normal-hearing people to listen to the hearing aid of a
hearing-impaired child.

HAL HEN COMPANY

Catalogue number: 787, Ear Level Testing Stethoscope

## DEVICES THAT KEEP AIDS, EARMOLDS, AND BATTERIES SAFE FROM HUMIDITY

HAL HEN COMPANY

Catalogue number: 270, Dri Aid Senior

## TELEVISION AMPLIFYING DEVICES

HAL HEN COMPANY

Catalogue number: 1095, Telex Sound Ear TV
        Unit—uses insert earphones

OR

Catalogue number: 537A, Marvel Inductor—to be used with telecoil
        switch on aid

Mid Audio Inc.

Catalogue number: 251, Phonear

Radio Shack

Catalogue number: 277-1008A, Archer 200mW
        Amplifier–Speaker

WITH

Catalogue number: 33–1058, Realistic Tie Clip Mike

### RADIOS THAT PICK UP TELEVISION SIGNALS
### (And Can Amplify Into Insert Earphones)

Panasonic
Sony
G.E.

Mid Audio Inc.

Catalogue number: 121 TV Band Radio

Radio Shack: Three Models

Portable (can go in Pocket)
(Includes weather band)

Portable radio size (AM-FM, TV, VHF band)

Portable radio size (AM-FM, TV)

*Karen L. Dilka*

# 5

# The Professionals and Others Who Work with the Hearing-Impaired Child in School

A network of specialists provides educational programming and services to the hearing-impaired student. These professionals are instrumental in the construction, development, and implementation of an individualized program. This educational program is designed to expand the student's knowledge and skills using a progressive, systematic format. Goals are set up for the student and the team specialists, which evolve from objectives identified for the student. The most significant goal is creating an atmosphere that facilitates academic achievement and will cultivate social/emotional adjustment.

The role of each specialist is defined in terms of specific tasks he or she is qualified to initiate and/or administer. In a program established for the hearing impaired, an overlapping of educational responsibilities will exist. This is due primarily to the emphasis placed on communication. The extensive speech and language deficits require intensive, continuous therapy. To apply such a concentrated theraputic plan, modifications are necessary in staff positions and duties. While minor alterations are made for incorporating communication skills throughout the academic environment, the basic function of each specialist remains unaltered. Consequently, the student benefits from additional support and reinforcement of progress in speech and language development.

THE HEARING-IMPAIRED CHILD IN SCHOOL
ISBN 0-8089-1663-7

This chapter will focus on the professionals involved in the educational evaluation, placement, and instruction of the hearing-impaired student. Collectively, the team promotes and encourages the development of a productive individual. Guidelines regarding activities and competencies to aid in the accomplishment of this objective are presented. Since parents participate in all aspects of educational decision-making concerning their child's comprehensive growth, they are a major component of the team. Therefore, a segment on parental influence and interaction is included.

## EDUCATORS OF THE ACOUSTICALLY HANDICAPPED

### Definition

"Educator of the acoustically handicapped" is a broad label used to describe teachers trained to provide instruction for the hearing impaired within an educational environment. Other interchangeable titles for the teachers are educator/teacher of the hearing impaired/deaf/aurally handicapped, or hearing handicapped. The general term encompasses three basic teaching categories: (1) the self-contained classroom teacher, (2) the resource hearing clinician, and (3) the itinerant hearing clinician. Many teachers do work in residential schools for the deaf, but that specialization is outside the scope of this chapter and text. Factors used to distinguish the three positions involved are (1) the amount of time scheduled for pupils, (2) the methodology of instruction provided, (3) the degree of required supplementary intervention, and (4) the number of students per caseload.

### Responsibilities

Several responsibilities pertain exclusively to the educator of the hearing impaired as a team member. First, an appropriate classroom environment conducive to learning must be established (Gonzales, Serwatka, & Van Nagel, 1977). Rapport building is an excellent tool used for this purpose. The desirable effect stimulates motivation and cooperation from the student. A second important function of the educator is adaptation of curriculum materials. Skill in material identification, evaluation, and organization enables the educator to enhance individual instruction, which is a priority in programming. Adjustment in activities, including utilization of group or individual aids and formulating new methods of teaching, are auxiliary procedures. Another responsibility of the educator is to foster the development of critical and creative thinking (Yater, 1977). Planning immediate and long-term goals will accommodate the development of these qualities. Lastly, guiding administrators in the selection of classroom teachers for the main-streamed hearing-impaired student helps in the avoidance of possible problem situations.

Educators of the hearing impaired must have cooperative relation-ships with all classroom teachers, administrators, nurses, librarians, and other support personnel. Continuous contact with parents regarding the student's skill level, behavior patterns, and advancement is an imper-ative duty. Maintenance of good public relations with other schools (public or private) and community agencies for hearing–handicapped persons increases the flow and exchange of materials and information.

*Educational Requirements*

Presently, the general requirement for employment in most states is a bachelor's degree from an accredited college or university with preparation in an educational training program for teachers of the hear-ing impaired/handicapped. Most are accredited by the Council on Ed-ucation of the Deaf. Many school districts require additional training, i.e., a master's degree during a person's tenure. Additional communi-cation skills such as competency in one or more sign language systems may be required, depending on the school district regulations, philos-ophy, and instructional methodology.

## Self-contained Classroom Teacher

*Definition*

A self-contained classroom refers to a setting where hearing-im-paired students, usually with profound losses, remain for educational purposes throughout an entire day. All academic subjects are taught within this framework except by special arrangement, i.e. physical ed-ucation.

*Responsibilities*

The teacher must have knowledge in numerous subject areas, in-tertwined with the ability to convey content information in an inter-esting, accurate manner. Preparation of the physical environment for precise visual and auditory reception before lesson presentation is nec-essary to ensure and enhance student comprehension, (Ross, Brackett, & Maxon, 1982).

The self-contained classroom teacher needs proficiency in which-ever mode of communication school policy dictates. If student pref-erence for understanding and clarification requires oral and manual methods, skill in both in mandatory. Inservice consultation with other staff members contributes effectively to the consistency of the com-munication approach.

Other significant duties entail the enrichment of receptive and ex-pressive language, the evaluation of academic success and failure, and the monitoring of developmental patterns. An awareness of the possible impact of relevant medical factors on these patterns is also essential (Martin, 1978), (Roeser & Downs, 1981).

## The Resource Clinician

### Definition

A hearing resource program serves all hearing-impaired students, whether their loss be mild or profound. Students in the program are seen at regularly scheduled times during the school day for supple-mental and supportive help. They are usually mainstreamed into regular classrooms during the remainder of the day. The characteristics of spe-cial needs among these students include defective speech, underde-veloped language patterns, reading problems, and socialization diffi-culties.

### Responsibilities

The responsibilities of the resource teacher to the hearing-impaired student includes daily assistance in the use of expressive and receptive speech and the development of language skills. These are enhanced through lipreading (speech reading), auditory training exercises, lan-guage and speech work, and a combination of materials and texts used in the permanent classroom. Guidance is provided for the student to aid in the achievement of social and emotional maturity. This includes independence and self-confidence to function comfortably in a class-room, (Bowman, 1973). The student should be encouraged to participate in class discussions, to ask for necessary help, and to learn to follow directions. Notetakers and interpreters are organized by the clinician for this purpose. Development of a student's positive self-image and a realistic idea of his or her abilities are significant responsibilities of the clinician.

The resource clinican also provides services to classroom teachers by reinforcing previously covered classroom information. Reviewing a particular assignment or lesson aids the student in learning and saves the classroom teacher valuable time. To ease classroom tension in reference to the student's hearing deficit, the clinician will distribute information or give presentations concerning hearing loss, hearing devices, and/or other related topics. Providing the teacher with a list of potential behaviors typically associated with a student who has a hearing loss heightens the awareness of the teacher in the identification process.

Orienting teachers to particular situations in which the student may have difficulties in functioning relieves unnecessary frustration for all concerned. A few helpful suggestions written specifically for the classroom teacher are discussed in Chapter 6.

Building positive attitudes and eliminating misconceptions are important for the success of the student.

## The Itinerant Hearing Clinician

*Definition*

Many similarities exist between the position of a resource and an itinerant clinician. Both focus on maximum individualized instruction and remediation through supportive services. Therefore, the responsibilities and duties are basically equivalent.

*Responsibilities*

Major differences between these two specialists involve the role, caseload, and time allotted for each student. First, an itinerant clinician serves more than one school. Often, this is due to the uneven distribution of hearing-impaired students throughout a school district. For example, there may be a few students in several schools, and none in others. For efficient use of facilities, the traveling clinician must establish a centrally located room in each school for instruction, storage of equipment, and materials. Secondly, the caseload of an itinerant clinician includes students whose hearing losses range from mild to profound, who have differing oral communications skills, and who are capable of performing in a regular classroom setting with intermittent supportive assistance. Lastly, time must be used effectively, since the clinician provides services throughout the school district. With a larger caseload than the resource clinician, the itinerant clinician frequently conducts group lessons as opposed to individual lessons in areas such as speech enhancement training, auditory training, communication and listening skills, reading and in academic areas. Diversity, time utilization and flexibility are key components in this situation.

**Tutor**

*Definition*

The tutor may be a teacher aide, adult, or peer who has expertise in a distinct subject matter area. A tutor must have excellent communication skills, using the preferred mode of the student, that is, oral or manual or both. In all instances, body language, sign language, speech articulation, and active listening must be employed. Although the purpose of tutoring is to explain or to clarify concepts in academic material, other principles of language should be simultaneously taught. Northcott (1973) suggests that the tutor should incorporate vocabulary expansion, abstract concept expansion, and the development of a sense of humor.

Establishing a healthy working relationship facilitates the exchange of information. By maintaining good rapport through the expression of positive regard, a student will feel comfortable asking questions. Empathy, sensitivity, and patience are qualities that nurture the reception of a tutor's performance by the student, (Osguthorpe, 1980), (Northcott, 1973).

*Responsibilities*

Duties synonymous with tutoring procedures include the use of visual and auditory aids (if appropriate) and consultation with teachers about assignments and materials. It is the responsibility of a tutor to encourage the student to think and act in an independent manner. Osguthorpe (1980) states that *guiding* a student to the correct response demonstrates tutoring skill. Requirements for employment are based on individual school system policy.

**Notetaker**

*Definition*

The hearing-impaired student encounters difficulty in classes where visual contact with the teacher must be maintained while concurrently taking notes. It is virtually impossible to read lips and write simultaneously. Notetakers are imperative, therefore, to a student's successful competion of course work.

*Responsibilities*

A notetaker is generally the student's peer and may or may not be enrolled in the class for credit. Common procedures involve the sharing of notes, photocopying the notes, or the use of carbon paper to duplicate the notes. Writing all information accurately and legibly are major priorities.

The following are practices and suggestions for developing good notes:

1. identify and record all principal points made by the teacher
2. determine and record secondary points
3. use headings and subheadings
4. organize the content logically
5. define difficult concepts and key words
6. date the notes daily
7. record all references, assignments, and due dates
8. recognize the importance of neatness and clarity, (Osguthorpe, 1980).

As with the tutor, employment is determined by school policy.

## Interpreter

*Role and Responsibilities*

The role, function, and responsibilities of an interpreter (oral and manual) are presented in Chapter 11.

## Audiologist

*Role and Responsibilities*

A school audiologist conducts comprehensive audiological evaluations on students who have or are suspected of having a hearing loss. Standard procedures administered during the routine assessment include pure–tone and speech threshold measurements and impedance audiometry. The audiologist closely monitors any fluctuation in hearing perception or variations in middle ear status, (Berg, 1976). Unusual changes may indicate the need for additional testing or referral to an appropriate physician. If the student is currently wearing a hearing aid, periodic performance checks are conducted, and earmold impressions are made. If a type of amplication is not being worn presently and an obvious need exists, referral for selection of an aid will follow testing, or the audiologist will evaluate for and fit the appropriate aid. The audiologist may be requested to perform other diagnostic evaluations, such as the auditory processing battery, when questionable behaviors appear in the classroom.

The rehabilitation aspects of audiology revolve around programs emphasizing maximum use of residual hearing. A considerable amount of aural stimulation is provided through auditory training sessions organized by the audiologist, (Oyer and Frankmann, 1975), (Schow and

Nerbonne, 1980). Ross and Calvert (1976) suggest that speech and language programs based on the auditory approach should be incorporated into the area of audiology also. These techniques, conducted by the audiologist, provide opportunities for a student to improve his or her lipreading and listening skills.

The acoustic characteristics of all classrooms must be monitored carefully for excessive environmental noise. Advising school administrators regarding possible techniques to eliminate distracting noise is a vital function of the audiologist. Another important duty is to supervise the use of amplifying equipment in the classroom. Obtaining knowledge about the selection, operation, and repair of these systems is important for proper maintenance, (Ross & Calvert, 1976).

Supervision of total audiological program services for the hearing-impaired student is a primary focus of the audiologist. Under the umbrella of audiology, several ongoing projects are of particular significance to the audiologist: (1) early identification; (2) hearing conservation workshops; and (3) student admission, placement, and staffing needs, (Berg, 1976). In addition to these duties the audiologist conducts in-service training for district personnel, in areas such as: (1) significance of the audiograms; (2) earmold care; (3) acoustics of speech; (4) trouble-shooting of hearing aids; (5) hints for classroom teachers; and (6) speech/language development techniques.

The role of the audiologist encompasses more than rudimentary screening, testing, and forms of consultation. Involvement with various components of the hearing-impaired community is an intricate part of facilitating awareness and gaining support for program goals. This participation is also shared by the other aforementioned professionals. Professional exchange of information with related fields of medicine, education, and social service agencies can provide a wealth of information, referrals, and community support.

A master's degree is required for employment in audiology. Additional information on requirements for certification may be obtained through the American Speech, Language, & Hearing Association. School systems determine whether national certification or state licensure is necessary in each individual district.

## Speech-Language Therapist

*Role and Responsibilities*

A comprehensive plan encompassing speech and language remediation is the responsibility of a speech-language pathologist. Effective screening methods for identification of speech and language disorders initiates the process of building an individualized program for the student. Information is then obtained concerning the etiology of the hearing impairment. If the loss has not been previously diagnosed, referral for an audiological assessment is generally recommended to the parent. The next step is a determination of the nature and severity of the impact of the hearing loss through diagnostic testing of all speech and language parameters. Articulation (production of sounds), voice characteristics (pitch, intensity, duration), and fluency (rate, rhythm) are the speech factors analyzed. Syntax, semantics, and the ability to understand contextual meaning are the language components examined. Strategies are then outlined to achieve the objectives established for speech/language correction and improvement.

A cooperative relationship between the speech therapist and student must evolve. This promotes motivation and stimulates the student to continue practicing newly acquired skills. Reinforcement of correct articulation, acceptable voice quality, and accurate language patterns encourages the student to expand his or her scope of communication (Eisenson & Ogilvie, 1971). With this result, a more positive self-image is generally projected.

Distribution of speech and language materials to the classroom teacher and parent will aid in the integration of these subjects throughout all phases of the student's educational process. In conjunction with providing these teaching resources, consultation and instruction for effective application are the speech-language pathologists' responsibilities. Incorporation of speech and language practice in all school settings increases the student's ability in developing improved communication skills.

Conducting workshops, counseling, and guidance for school personnel, parents, and students are all ingredients in the role of a speech-language pathologist. Active community participation is necessary to promote an exchange of ideas, materials, and equipment. New methods for program enrichment may also be obtained from these community sources.

A master's degree is required for school employment. Additional information regarding certification may be acquired through the American Speech, Language, & Hearing Association.

## Psychologist

*Role and Responsibilities*

The primary responsibility of a school psychologist is to provide hearing-impaired students and their parents with professional support and personal guidance, (Gerken, Grimes, & Brown, 1978, Cantor-Spragins, 1977). Of equal importance is the provision of evaluations, including either performance, aptitude, or personality. These assessments will aid school staff in planning a student's educational goals/curriculum.

School psychologists work with the entire school population; however, the hearing-impaired student presents a unique challenge. The difficulties center around speech and language development, social awareness, and the ramifications of the communication barrier. Psychologists must take these intrinsic realities into consideration or they will grossly misinterpret test results. Being cognizant of the total effect that delayed and restricted language has on performance outcome, being aware of the norming groups used for comparison, and possessing knowledge of appropriate test selections are critical considerations, (Bolton, 1976).

The underlying factor in the rapport building process between the psychologist and the hearing-impaired student is *communication*. A misunderstanding can skew any attempts of personal or academic problem resolution. A psychologist must be aware of limitations that he or she may possess as it relates to communication with the hearing impaired, and should request assistance if necessary in this area. In most instances, a manual or oral interpreter is available. Other outside professional consultation, especially with experts on hearing impairment, will be extremely beneficial for all involved.

Requirements for employment in an educational setting fluctuate between a master's degree in psychology and a doctorate degree. A psychologist involved with the hearing impaired should also have communication skills commensurate with that population. The American Psychological Association provides information on certification requirements of all psychologists.

## The Social Worker

*Role and Responsibilities*

The social worker becomes involved in a student's educational process when governmental intervention or counseling assistance is advisable. Generally, the dynamics involving social worker mitigation entail a family crisis or problems. Financial difficulties may also interfere with the student's educational development, therefore requiring funding/aid. The social worker provides guidance, support, and assistance in all these areas.

Follow-up and continued supervision are extremely important. Therefore, the role of the social worker may be long-term. The responsibility of continual periodic interaction with the student establishes a monitoring system. Pertinent information can then be coordinated among academic, governmental, and parental arenas for enhancement of the student's educational pursuits.

Depending on the job qualifications outlined by individual school systems, a bachelor's or master's degree may be required for employment. In many instances, an emphasis in child and family counseling may be necessary.

## The Classroom Teacher

*Role and Responsibilities*

The role of the classroom teacher consists of imparting academic information/knowledge to students. This general responsibility is comprised of many specific duties. First, a positive, enthusiastic attitude toward learning must be generated. An atmosphere fostering acceptance and respect creates an exceptional opportunity for social and academic growth, (Northcott, 1973). Another important task conducted by the classroom teacher is to select teaching materials that will facilitate the hearing-impaired student's mastery of subject matter, (Davis, 1977). A prior evaluation of the individual's proficiencies and limitations provides a basis for activity and lesson planning. Visual aids should be chosen that clarify the concept being taught. Additionally, the teacher must confer regularly with parents and other professionals to inform them about the progress and status of the hearing-impaired student.

Davis, (1977) indicates that as a result of the increased movement toward mainstreaming, hearing-impaired students are attending schools in which classroom teachers may have had no previous exposure to deafness or experience in teaching these students. Therefore, orientation and continuous consultation by a specialist in the area of deafness is imperative. Teachers encountering this situation need to become aware of significant details that will enhance the student's learning process. Examples include appropriate seating arrangements, hearing aid usage, lip reading contingencies, and special services that are available. An indepth list of helpful hints has been prepared in Chapter 6.

## Administrator

*Role and Responsibilities*

A school administrator's primary responsibility is to supervise the enforcement of public law/policy within the educational environment.

The administrator must be informed about current legislation and possible ramifications for the hearing impaired. Another related aspect is funding. Therefore, knowledge of procedures for obtaining federal, state, and local aid is mandatory. Program/service development and maintenance stems from sufficient monetary aid. Interfaced with financial awareness is realistic budget planning to ensure appropriate standards are met for support services.

The position of administrator also entails guidance and coordination of staff specialists. Although he or she is the school authority regarding overall program development, most determinations are based on consultation with involved team members. Scheduling, discipline, and placement are examples where input from the staff is vital. Skillful leadership by a school administrator contributes to staff enthusiasm and program success.

## Parents

### Role and Responsibilities

Realizing that parents are the primary influence in a child's life, their inclusion as team members becomes mandatory. Parents contribute a vast amount of information concerning the child's medical, emotional, psychological, and social status. This knowledge is vital for planning an individualized program. Their involvement and cooperation are key elements to the student's successful program completion.

Parental expectations and goals established for a hearing-impaired child should be realistic. Several dynamics must be considered, such as the degree of impairment, etiology, onset of loss, and communication skills. Awareness of the child's potential, as well as his or her limitations, allows the child to develop within a flexible framework.

### Suggestions for Parents

Suggestions for effective communication between a parent and child with a hearing impairment follow. Although many more could be added to this list, these represent some of the most significant.

- Be patient, encouraging, understanding, and supportive.
- Explain all relevant situations and events.
- Provide the child with his or her own responsibilities.
- Use the child's preferred mode of communication.
- Set behavioral limits and use consistent discipline.
- Utilize the child's residual hearing.
- Assist with academic assignments.

It is important for parents to remember that as role models, their attitudes (positive and negative) are conveyed to the child. A child's adaptation into a specified classroom may be contingent on the reactions expressed by the parents. Therefore, a major responsibility off parents is to communicate their values, thoughts, and ideas in a direct, understandable manner.

## CONCLUSION

These professionals combine their talents to facilitate the learning process for hearing-impaired students. They initiate and administer a creative program revolving around academic achievement, social awareness, and emotional maturity. This approach utilizes the function, knowledge, role, and responsibilities of each member to promote positive growth in all aspects of the student's development.

## REFERENCES

Berg, F.S. Educational audiology. New York: Grune and Stratton, 1976.

Bolton, B. The psychology of deafness for rehabilitation counselors Baltimore: University Park Press, 1976.

Bowman, E. A resource room program for hearing impaired students. The Volta Review, 1973, 75, 208-215.

Cantor, D.W., & Spragins, A. Delivery of psychological services to the hearing impaired child in the elementary school. American Annals of the Deaf, 1977, 122,330-336.

Davis, J. (Ed.). Our forgotten children: Hard-of-hearing pupils in the schools. Minneapolis, Minnesota: U.S. Office of Education, 1977.

Eisenson, J., & Ogilvie, M. Speech correction in the schools. New York: Macmillan Publishing Co., Inc., 1971.

Gerken, K., Grimes, J., & Brown, J. A step forward: Psychological services to children who are hearing impaired. American Annals of the Deaf, 1978, 123, 448-451.

Gonzales, R., Serwatka, T.S., & Van Nagel, C. A model evaluation system for use in a competency based teacher evaluation program in hearing impairment. American Annals of the Deaf, 1977, 122, 492-503.

Martin, F. N. Pediatric audiology. Englewood Cliffs, New Jersey: Prentice-Hall Inc., 1978.

Northcott, W.H. (Ed.). The hearing impaired child in a regular classroom: Preschool, elementary, and secondary years. Washington, D.C.: The Alexander Graham Bell Association for the Deaf, 1973.

Osguthorpe, R.T. The tutor/notetaker. Washington, D.C.: The Alexander Graham Bell Association for the Deaf, 1980.

Oyer, H.J., & Frankmann, J.P. The aural rehabilitation process. New York: Holt, Rinehart, and Winston, 1975.

Roeser, R., & Downs, M., (Eds.). Auditory disorders in school children the law. identification. remediation. New York: Thieme-Stratton, Inc., 1081.

Ross, M., Brackett, D., & Maxon, A. Hard of hearing children in the public schools. New Jersey: Prentice-Hall Inc., 1982.

Ross, M., & Calvert, D.R. Guidelines for audiology programs in educational settings for hearing impaired children. *American Annals of the Deaf*, 1976, *121*, 346-350.

Schow, R.L., & Nerbonne, M.A. (Eds.). *Introduction to aural rehabilitation*. Baltimore: University Park Press, 1980.

Van Hattum R.J. (Ed.) *Speech-Language programming in the schools*. Springfield, Illinois: Charlies C. Thomas, 1982.

Yater, V.V. *Mainstreaming of children with a hearing loss*. Springfield, Illinois: Charles C. Thomas, 1982.

## BIBLIOGRAPHY

American Speech and Hearing Association. *Guidelines for identification audiometry*. Washington, D.C.: Author, 1975.

American Speech and Hearing Association. *Standards and guidelines for comprehensive language, speech, and hearing programs in the schools*. Washington, D.C.: Author, 1973–1974.

Bitter, G.B. (Ed.) *Parents in action, handbook of experiences with their hearing impaired children*. Washington, D.C.: Alexander Graham Bell association for the Deaf, 1978.

Council on Education of the Deaf. *Standards for the certification of teachers of the hearing impaired*. Rochester, New York: Author, 1972.

Giangreco, C.J., & Giangreco, M.R. *The Education of the Hearing Impaired*. Springfield, Illinois: Charles C. Thomas, Publisher, 1976.

Hehir, R.G. Competence based teacher education for teachers of the deaf: the issues from the state level. *The Volta Review*, 1975, 77, 105–116.

Joint Committee of American Speech and Hearing Association and Conference of Executives of American Schools for the Deaf. Guidelines for audiology programs in educational settings for hearing impaired children. *ASHA*, 1976, *18*, 291–294.

Katz, L., Mathis, S.L., III, & Merrill, E.C., Jr. *The deaf child in the public schools*. Danville, Illinois: Interstate Printers and Publishers, 1979.

Nix, G.W. (Ed.). *Mainstream education for hearing impaired children and youth*. New York: Grune and Stratton, 1976.

Shane, H.C., & Yoder, D.E. Delivery of augmentative communication services: the role of the speech-language pathologist. *Language, Speech and Hearing Services in Schools*, 1981, *12*, 211–215.

Subtelny, J.D. (Ed.). *Speech assessment and speech improvement for the hearing impaired*. Washington, D.C.: Alexander Graham Bell Association for the Deaf, 1980.

Turnbull, A.P., & Turnbull, H.R. *Parents speak out*. Columbus, Ohio: Charles E. Merrill, 1978.

*Charlene M. Kampfe*

# 6

# Placement and Programming for the Hearing-Impaired Child in School

The education of hearing-impaired children formally began in the United States in 1817 when the first school for the deaf was established in Hartford, Connecticut. Unique features of this school included enrollment of both in-state and out-of-state students, provision of residential quarters, use of manual communication, and consultation with other states that wished to establish similar schools (Berger, 1972; Moores, 1982). Since that beginning, many other types of educational settings and programs have been developed to serve students with hearing impairments.

The purpose of this chapter is to inform the reader of the types of educational settings that are presently available. The chapter will discuss some of the advantages and disadvantages of these settings, and will present research findings regarding their relationships to academic achievement, communication skills, psychosocial development, and use of hearing aids. Important criteria for determining whether an individual child will benefit from a mainstreamed program will also be presented.

## EDUCATIONAL SETTINGS

Educational programs are often categorized according to the degree to which hearing-impaired children are integrated with normally hearing children (Brill, 1974; Karchmer & Trybus, 1977; Quigley & Kretschmer, 1982; Reich, Hambleton & Houldin, 1977). Although classification systems differ among professionals, educational settings are often divided into two categories: (1) integrated and (2) segregated.

### Integrated Settings

Integrated settings can generally be described as those that place hearing-impaired children in classes or schools with normally hearing children. Another term that is often used interchangeably with integration is *mainstreaming*. These program settings are most often associated with municipal schools rather than with residential facilities or with private, parochial schools (Craig, Salem, & Craig, 1976).

The number of hearing-impaired children enrolled in integrated settings, as defined in this chapter, has steadily increased in the past 35 years (Moores, 1982). Findings regarding the percentages of students in these programs have been somewhat stable in recent years. Both Karchmer and Trybus (1977) and Craig and Craig (1980) found that approximately 41 percent of the educational placements of hearing-impaired students in the United States were accounted for in integrated settings. Rawlings and Trybus (1978) found that integrated settings accounted for a slightly larger proportion of enrollments (47 percent); however, these inconsistencies are likely to be related to different definitions used by the three research groups. More recently, Craig and Craig (1982) found that approximately 50 percent of the hearing-impaired children in the United States were placed in integrated settings.

Integrated programs span a broad range of degrees of integration. The following presents a continuum of these program settings from fully integrated to partially segregated (Brill, 1974; Craig et al., 1976; McGee, 1976; Reich et al., 1977):

FULLY INTEGRATED I.   The student is completely integrated into a normally hearing classroom of a regular school. No special support services are given. This type of mainstreaming appears to occur less frequently than other forms of integration (Craig et al., 1976).

FULLY INTEGRATED II.   The student is placed in a normally hearing classroom of a regular school, but has outside support services, such as (1) an itinerant teacher who travels from school to school providing tutoring and special services to individual hearing-impaired students,

(2) an interpreter–tutor who attends classes with the student, and (3) a resource room where the student has access to a specially trained teacher who provides for the special educational needs of a number of disabled students in the school. These types of programs appear to be more prevalent than others (Karchmer & Trybus, 1977).

PARTIALLY INTEGRATED I.   The student is placed in a classroom with both normally hearing children and hearing-impaired children. Team teachers, one qualified to work with hearing-impaired children and one qualified to teach normally hearing children, share the teaching responsibilities.

PARTIALLY INTEGRATED II.   The student is placed in a special classroom for hearing-impaired students, but attends some academic classes with normally hearing students (i.e., mathematical computation or other classes not requiring a great deal of verbal interaction).

PARTIALLY SEGREGATED I.   The student is placed in a self-contained classroom with hearing-impaired students, but attends nonacademic classes and/or activities with the normally hearing students of the school (i.e., vocational, art, physical education).

PARTIALLY SEGREGATED II.   The student is placed in a completely self—contained classroom for the hearing impaired, with only occasional contact with normally hearing students of the school (i.e., recess, lunch).

This list is not exhaustive of all integrated settings offered today. It is, however, a summary of the types of integrated settings most often used. The Partially Segregated I and Partially Segregated II settings might also have been listed with segregated programs. They have been included with integrated programs, however, because they are more commonly found in regular schools than in day or residential schools.

The more fully integrated programs listed above have been found to serve a different group of hearing-impaired students than programs that are less integrated. Generally, they tend to serve children with more mild or moderate hearing losses, higher family education and income, and a lower incidence of prelingual hearing loss (loss before age 3) (Karchmer & Trybus, 1977). They also serve a smaller number of children with hearing-impaired parents than segregated settings serve (Karchmer, Trybus, & Paquin, Note 1).

Depending upon the orientation of the school, integrated programs use a variety of methods of instruction, ranging from oral-aural methods to total communication.

Oral-aural methods can generally be described as those that stress the use of functional speech, speech reading, amplification, auditory training, reading, and writing to minimize the effects of the disability. Although there are a variety of oral-aural methods, most adhere to the same basic philosophy. They typically support the notion that manual communication may adversely affect the development of oral communication skills, and that it should therefore not be used (Berger, 1972; Moores, 1982).

Total communication can be described as an educational philosphy that stresses using any methods of communication that are effective with the individual. These methods include speech, speech reading, made-up signs, sign language, finger spelling, pantomine, reading, amplification, and writing (Alexander, 1978; Berger, 1972; Moores, 1982). Further discussion of this philosophy can be found in Chapter 11.

## Segregated Settings

Segregated settings are those that offer little or no contact between hearing-impaired students and normally hearing students. These settings tend to serve children with more severe losses, a higher incidence of prelingual hearing impairment, and lower family education and income (Karchmer & Trybus, 1977). They also serve a greater number of children with hearing-impaired parents than integrated settings serve (Karchmer, et al., Note 1). The proportion of students enrolled in segregated settings appears to have decreased in the past few years. In 1980, Craig and Craig reported that 56 percent of the total population of hearing-impaired students in the United States were enrolled in these settings. In 1982, this percentage had decreased to 48 percent (Craig & Craig, 1982).

Two basic types of programs are typically associated with these settings: (1) residential schools for the deaf, and (2) day schools for the hearing impaired. These programs can be private or public and are sometimes associated with programs for the visually impaired.

RESIDENTIAL SCHOOLS FOR THE DEAF. Residential schools for the deaf are educational institutions located on campuses that include dormitories, administration buildings, classroom buildings, gymnasiums, and cafeterias. They offer a full range of special services from grades 1 through 12. Some have developed special preschool programs as well. Enrollments range from approximately 100 to 700 students, and students come from throughout the state (Craig & Craig, 1982). These residential schools have been estimated to account for 37 percent (Craig & Craig, 1982) to 39 percent (Craig & Craig, 1980) of the total school enrollment of hearing-impaired students in the United States. They typically adhere to the total communication philosophy of instructing hearing-impaired children.

Although these schools are called residential, they also serve students who live at home with their families. In more recent years, the number of children who commute from home to school has increased considerably. In 1978, Rawlings and Trybus estimated this figure to be from 15 percent to 20 percent of all residential school students. This figure increased to approximately 30 percent in the 1981–1982 school year (Craig & Craig, 1982).

There appear to be some differences in characteristics between these commuter students and those who live on campus. Karchmer and Petersen (1980) found that children who live at home are more likely to be from families of a higher economic level than those who are in residence. They also found that many more white than black students commute between school and home.

DAY SCHOOLS FOR THE HEARING IMPAIRED.    Day schools are usually located in large, metropolitan areas. They are typically self-contained units providing a segregated education to hearing-impaired students (Quigley & Kretschmer, 1982). The proportion of students attending day schools has fluctuated. In 1977, Karchmer and Trybus found that 11 percent attended such schools. Three years later, Craig and Craig (1980) found this percentage to increase to 17 percent. In a more recent study, Craig and Craig (1982) found the percentage of students attending day schools to drop to 11 percent of the total enrollment.

Although residential and day schools are usually segregated programs, they do not always have total segregation. Craig et al. (1982) found that approximately 4 percent of residential students and 25 percent of day school students were reported to be enrolled in mainstreamed or partially mainstreamed programs.

## ADVANTAGES AND DISADVANTAGES OF INTEGRATED AND SEGREGATED PROGRAMS

Sorting through the advantages and disadvantages of each type of educational setting can be confusing. Certainly, there is not full agreement among professionals. This section will attempt to present various points of view that have been suggested in the available literature.

Many of the following statements regarding the advantages and disadvantages of the various settings have not been substantiated through careful research. Many are opinions that may or may not be accurate. For this reason, one must view them with caution, using a critical point of reference when considering them.

## Integrated Settings

One of the primary advantages of an integrated setting is thought to be the child's ability to live at home. Living with the family allows the child to establish ongoing sibling and parental relationships, to learn the feeling and meaning of being a part of a family, and to have the opportunity to observe parents as role models (Brill, 1974; Gonzales, 1980; Moores, 1982).

Integration gives the child the opportunity to interact with the hearing world. Living in the hearing community and attending regular schools is expected to help him or her develop normal, noninstitutional social and vocational behaviors and attitudes (Brill, 1978; Craig et al., 1976; McHugh, 1975).

Teachers in integrated settings have indicated that mainstreaming contributes to the children's development of communication skills (Brill, 1978; Craig et al., 1976). It is thought that students in integrated settings will be more likely to use their residual hearing and to develop normal speaking and speech reading skills because of the need to rely on these methods of communication (Courtman-Davies, 1979).

Along with the benefits to the individual child, integration has been thought to bring an awareness to the public of the problems of deafness and ,thus, greater acceptance of persons with this disability (Brill, 1978; Gonzales, 1980).

Vernon and Prickett (1976), on the other hand, have indicated that early mainstreamed programs failed to serve hearing-impaired students because they were inappropriately implemented. They stated that schools failed to modify curriculum, to provide socioemotional support, and to sensitize teachers and other students to the needs of hearing-impaired students. These problems may apply to today's mainstreamed programs. Brill (1974) warns that regular schools attempting to offer day class programs to hearing-impaired children may not have large enough numbers of these students to provide for their needs. He argues that these children may be placed in special classrooms of dissimilar oral abilities, chronological ages, mental ages, and educational levels without regard for individual needs.

Perhaps the primary disadvantage of an integrated program is the potential failure to provide the necessary special support services needed by hearing-impaired children. Principals and supervising teachers of these integrated schools are often not familiar with deafness. Specialists such as psychologists, audiologists, speech therapists, nurses, interpreters, and special teachers who are familiar with deafness and who are able to communicate with deaf children are not always available in intergrated programs. This lack of expertise may result in little or no guidance for the regular classroom teacher who is attempting to provide an education to the hearing-impaired child (Brill, 1974, 1978; Gonzales, 1980).

In a national study of 12 of the larger mainstreamed programs, Brill (1978) found few deaf models for hearing-impaired children to observe. He also found that teachers would sometimes either inflate the grades of deaf students or require more of them because they were receiving services that normally hearing children were not receiving. Brill found that nearly all deaf children were socially overwhelmed during the first 6 months of integration, and that if the students did not have outgoing personalities, they often continued to have socialization programs (p. 177).

## Segregated Settings

The primary advantage of a residential school is the concentration of qualified staff to work with children who have hearing impairments. Such settings typically offer audiologists, audiometrists, speech therapists, social workers, nurses, guidance counselors, secretaries, administrative staff, and teachers specifically trained to work with persons with this disability (Quigley & Kretschmer, 1982; Rawlings & Trybus, 1978).

In residential schools, students have the opportunity to interact with counselors, teachers, and students with similar disabilities and communication modes (Liben, 1978). This allows them to share common problems, to feel more like their peers, and to observe and interact with hearing-impaired adult models (Brill, 1978).

Residential schools provide students with the opportunity to participate fully in all the social and athletic activities of the school without feeling that their disability is a handicap to their involvement (Quigley & Kretschmer, 1982). These schools also provide more extensive vocational services than mainstreamed programs (Rawlings & Trybus, 1978).

Perhaps the greatest disadvantage of being a student in residence is the child's separation from the family and the general population. Another disadvantage is the rigid structure of institutional life. Children are not always given opportunities to accept responsibility, to explore their environment, to evaluate themselves in relation to their normally hearing peers, to become familiar with the rules and mores of noninstitutionalized students their age, to experience normal interactions with the opposite sex, to develop prevocational skills necessary to survive in the hearing world, to observe parental models, or to experience being an active family member (Brill, 1974; Evans, 1975; Liben, 1978; McHugh, 1975; Meadow, 1978; Quigley & Kretschmer, 1982). In recent years, administrators have attempted to remedy some of these problems by requiring that children return to their homes on weekends and holidays (Meadow, 1978), and by encouraging daily commuting for children whose families live near the school.

Day schools appear to share the advantages of both integrated settings and residential settings. As in integrated settings, day school students live with their families and have the opportunity to interact with the hearing community. As in residential settings, day school students will have the opportunity to interact with others who share similar disabilities, will be more likely to have access to qualified staff, and will be able to participate fully in school activities.

A disadvantage of day schools might have to do with socialization. Because most of the day school students' neighborhood peers will be hearing children from public schools, some difficulty may be experienced in achieving close friendships during after-school hours. Another potential problem might occur when the school population is so small that students of varying ages, oral abilities, and educational levels are taught together rather than in homogeneous classrooms (Brill, 1974).

## RELATIONSHIPS BETWEEN SETTINGS AND SPECIFIC ASPECTS OF THE CHILD'S LIFE

Another way to examine the differences between integrated and segregated settings is to compare them on the basis of important areas of the hearing-impaired child's life. Four of these areas will be reviewed: academic achievement, psychosocial development, oral communication skills (speech intelligibility and speech reading), and use of hearing aids.

When reviewing research that compares various educational settings, significant differences in the above areas do not necessarily imply that one setting is superior to another. As noted earlier, students with different characteristics tend to be enrolled in different school settings (Karchmer & Trybus, 1977). These characteristics, rather than the school settings, may result in differences in academic achievement, psychosocial development, communication skills, and the use of hearing aids. For this reason, one must be cautioned against evaluating the effectiveness of the various programs based on any differences found between these students without considering other variables that might also affect these children.

### Academic Achievement

When reviewing research regarding academic achievement and school settings, one must recall that students from integrated and segregated settings differ from each other with regard to the hearing status of parents, degree of hearing loss, age at onset, socioeconomic level, and multihandicapping conditions. Since all these characteristics have been found to have some degree of relationship to academic achievement (DiFrancesca, 1972; Jensema, 1975, Ousley, 1974; Trybus & Karchmer, 1977), any differences between students from these program settings will likely be the result of complex interactions among all these variables rather than solely the influence of the settings.

Research findings consistently show a significant differnece in academic achievement between hearing-impaired children who have been in integrated settings and those who have not. These differences are more pronouced in reading achievement than in math achievement (Reich et al., 1977; Ries, 1973).

Students who attend integrated programs typically receive higher scores in academic achievement tests than those who have attended segregated programs (Jensema, 1975; van den Horst, 1971). Similarly, those who have attended special programs for the deaf on a part-time basis usually receive higher scores than those who have attended such programs on a full-time basis (Jensema, 1975; Ries, 1973). It is doubtful that the lower scores for full-time students are totally the result of the programs themselves, but rather of the characteristics of the students who were in need of full-time services.

When comparing students from various types of integrated settings, students in more fully integrated settings (i.e., itinerant programs and regular classrooms with minimal support services) tend to receive significantly higher academic scores than those who are in less integrated settings (i.e., full-time special education classes in a regular school setting) (Jensema, 1975; Reich et al., 1977). These differences are also likely to be closely related to the characteristics of the students enrolled in these programs.

Comparisons among segregated settings are somewhat different. Although residential school students who live at home appear to differ in several ways from those who live at the schools (i.e., ethnic bachground, economic level), they do not appear to differ with regard to academic achievement (Karchmer & Petersen, 1980; Quigley and Frisina, 1961).

When comparing students who attend day schools to students who attend residential schools, those attending the residential schools have been found to receive higher scores (Jensema, 1975). Jensema has speculated that the differences in academic achievement may have been related to the greater number of multidiabled students who were attending the day schools at that time (Gentile & McCarthy, 1973).

## Psychosocial Development

*Psychosocial development* is a broad term that is used to include social behavior, social integration, social acceptance, self-concept, emotional maturity, personality traits, and virtually all types of psychological and social aspects observed among hearing-impaired children.

Caution should be exercised when reviewing the results of studies regarding the psychosocial development of hearing-impaired children. Tests requiring a high degree of reading/language competence and/or subjective teacher and parent evaluations are often used to establish children's levels of development in this area. The results of these evaluations may not be valid. Instead of testing social maturity, psychological adjustment, or self-concept, researchers might be evaluating children's reading levels or parents' and teachers' attitudes toward deafness.

While students in integrated settings tend to receive higher academic achievement scores than students in segregated settings, the opposite is true with psychosocial development. With few exceptions (Kennedy, Northcott, McCauley, & Williams 1976; Sarfaty & Katz, 1978), research has consistently shown that hearing-impaired students in more fully segregated settings receive more positive psychosocial ratings than those who are involved in more fully integrated settings (Craig et al., 1977; Elser, 1959; Farrugia & Austin, 1980; van den Horst, 1971; Reich et al., 1977; Rister, 1975; Shears & Jensema, 1969).

In studying the differences between students of residential schools who reside at the school and those who commute, no significant differences have been found in psychosocial development (Quigley & Frisina, 1961).

## Oral Communication Skills

When reviewing the research regarding oral communication skills (speech and speech reading), it must be noted that students in more integrated settings tend to possess less severe degrees of hearing losses than those in more segregated settings (Karchmer & Trybus, 1977; Reich et al., 1977; Savafty & Katz, 1978). Students with these less severe losses likewise tend to achieve higher scores in oral communication than those with more severe losses. (moores, Weiss, & Goodwin, 1974; Reich et al., 1977). It is also important to note that students with better speech and speech reading skills may be more likely, in turn to be placed in integrated settings. For these reasons, it is possible that any differences in speech and speech reading between children of different program settings might be due to the *type* of student enrolled in the program rather than the *effect* of the program.

As a group, integrated students tend to have more intelligible speech than those in segregated settings (Karchmer & Trybus, 1977). When comparing varying degrees of integrated programs, Reich et al. (1977) found a decline in speech intelligibility and speech reading ability as the programs became less integrated. They also found that the longer students remained in integrated programs, the better their speech intelligibility became. This might be an indication that integrated programs contribute to improved speech and speech reading skills.

When comparing subgroups of segregated settings (i.e., day school students and/or day students of residential school students), findings have been consistent. Although the differences are not always statistically significant, day students tend to have better oral skills than residential students (Karchmer & Peterson, 1980; Klopping, 1972; Quigley & Frising, 1961).

## Use of Hearing Aids

In comparing the number of hearing aids worn by children in segregated versus integrated settings, one should not overlook the degree of deafness of the students enrolled in these programs. Because hearing aids seem to offer more benefit to children in the middle ranges of hearing impairment, whether one agrees with the philosophy or not, the use of an aid is often dependent upon the degree of hearing loss. Children with either "mild" or "profound" losses are less likely to wear aids than children with "moderate" or "severe" losses (Karchmer & Kirwin, 1977; Moores, 1982; Shepard, Davis, Gorga, & Stelmachowicz, 1981).

Students who reside in residential schools are less likely to wear hearing aids than any other group (Karchmer & Kirwin, 1977; Karchmer & Petersen, 1980; Karchmer & Trybus, 1977). Since these settings tend to enroll students with more profound losses, this lack of use may be partially explained by the type of students they serve. One might expect, however, that because of the more confined environment and the monitoring that could take place, that those who could benefit from amplification would be using it.

The next group that is least likely to wear hearing aids is composed of students who attend the more fully integrated programs (i.e., full-time integration, part-time special education classes, itinerant programs, resource rooms) (Karchmer & Kirwin, 1977; Karchmer & Trybus, 1977). A possible explanation may be that this group tends to have more "mild" hearing losses than students in other education settings (Karchmer & Trybus, 1977). This lack of use of amplification would be strongly argued against by those who feel that no matter how mild the hearing loss, if it is resulting in reduced educational functioning, amplification should be appropriately fit and implemented into each child's daily routine.

## CRITERIA FOR ENROLLMENT INTO AN INTEGRATED SETTING

The effectiveness of each type of educational setting will depend upon many factors. Degree of hearing loss, age at onset of loss, ability to speak and speech read, intelligence level, and personality characteristics are examples of internal variables that will affect the child's success or failure in an educational setting. External variables such as attitudes of parents, teachers, and fellow students; methods of communication used by the child and others; amount of support from parents; and hearing status of parents will also affect the child's success.

Because many variables are involved, no single setting is most effective for all hearing-impaired children. A number of professionals have noted that children who are successful in mainstreamed programs tend to have characteristics that relate to their success in that type of educational format. Presented below is a list of those characteristics that are most often found in successful mainstreamed students and, therefore, most often recommended as criteria for acceptance into these programs:

1. Normal to highly developed speech and speech reading skills (Craig, et al., 1976; Courtman-Davies, 1979; McConnell & Liff, 1975; Northcott, 1973; O'Conner, 1967; Pflaster, 1980; Reich et al., 1977).
2. Personality traits that include independence, social maturity, determiniation, high motivation, ability to accept criticism, positive self-concept, confidence, social skills that are similar to normally hearing children in the regular classroom, outgoing personality, and a positive attitude toward school and toward being enrolled in an integrated setting (Brill, 1978; Courtman-Davies, 1979; Craig et al., 1976; McConnell & Liff, 1975; Northcott, 1973; O'Conner, 1967; Pflaster, 1980; Reich et al., 1977).
3. Supportive parents who have accepted the hearing loss and the hearing aid, treat their child like the other children in the family, give affection freely, have actively requested enrollment in an integrated setting, have high expectations of their child, and are willing to be actively involved in the educational process (Brill, 1978; Courtman-Davies, 1979; Craig et al., 1976; O'Conner, 1967; Pflaster, 1980; Reich et al., 1977; Teller, 1975).
4. Average or above intelligence as measured by a standardized test (Brill, 1978; Courtman-Davies, 1979; Northcott, 1973; O'Conner, 1967; Reich et al., 1977).

5. Able to use the English language (reading, writing, and speaking) at or near the skill level of the other children in the regular classroom. The student should have the ability to paraphrase, to use English idioms, and to generate and vary sentence structure at the level of hearing peers (Northcott, 1973; O'Conner, 1967; Pflaster, 1980).
6. Academic skills that are within the normal range of the normally hearing children in regular classrooms (Craig et al., 1976; Northcott, 1973).
7. Optimal use of residual hearing and full-time use of a hearing aid when appropriate (Northcott, 1973; Pflaster, 1980).
8. Early intervention, which has helped the child develop the skills and traits listed above. Such intervention includes early evaluation and ongoing therapy services at speech and hearing clinics, early use of amplification, and early preschool or correspondence courses for language stimulation (Brill, 1978; McConnel & Liff, 1975; O'Connor, 1967).
9. Degree of loss. O'Connor (1967) suggested in an earlier report that only students with losses of less than 60-70dB should be enrolled in integrated settings. Reich et al (1967) suggest that students with greater degrees of losses can be enrolled, but will need more support services than children with less severe losses. Pflaster (1980), on the other hand, found in a more recent study that the degree of hearing loss did not seem to have an effect on children's academic successes in integrated settings.
10. Small family unit. The sibling constellation may have an impact on the success of hearing-impaired students in integrated settings. Those with smaller families have been found to attain higher academic achievement levels than those with larger families (Pflaster, 1980). This variable may be closely inter-related to the amount of time parents are able to give to their children in home assignments, speech and speech reading exercises, and natural parenting.

## SUMMARY

Hearing-impaired students should be thought of as individuals having individual educational needs. To ensure that they receive an education commensurate with their capabilities and characteristics, it is important that they be considered separately and that a variety of options be made available to them.

The types of options that exist today range from residential school settings to full-time integrated settings. To date, there is little conclusive evidence that one program is better than another. There is, however, some evidence that children with certain characteristics do not achieve as well as others in mainstreamed programs. Because of this, criteria have been suggested for entrance into such programs.

To determine which setting will be most appropriate, each child must be evaluated in relation to a number of variables. These include oral communication skills; personality traits; intelligence level; ability to use the English language; academic achievement level; use of residual hearing; degree and type of hearing loss and its effect on the child's ability to function; the child's attitude toward different school settings; parental support and desires; and any additional handicapping conditions. These characteristics, analyzed separately and together, should then be considered when selecting the educational setting for the child.

## REFERENCES

Alexander, K. R. Forgotten aspects of total communication. *American Annals of the Deaf,* 1978, *123,* 18–21.

Berger, K. W. *Speechreading principles and methods.* Baltimore: National Educational Press, Inc., 1972.

Brill, R. G. *The education of the deaf: administrative and professional development.* Washington, D.C.: Gallaudet College Press, 1974.

Brill, R. G. *Mainstreaming the prelingually deaf child.* Washington, D.C.: Gallaudet College Press, 1978.

Courtman-Davies, M. *Your deaf child's speech and language.* London: The Bodley Head, 1979.

Craig, W., & Craig, H. Directory of services for the deaf. *American Annals of the Deaf,* 1980, *125,* 179.

Craig, W. N., & Craig, H. B. Programs and Services for the Deaf in the United States. *American Annals of the Deaf,* 1982, *127,* 107–158.

Craig, W. N., Salem, J. M, & Craig, J. B. Mainstreaming and partial integration of deaf with hearing students. *American Annals of the Deaf,* 1976, *121.* 63–68.

DiFrancesca, S. *Academic achievement test results of a national testing program for hearing impaired students. United States: Spring, 1971* (Report Number 9, Series D.) Washington, D.C.: Gallaudet College, Office of Demographic Studies, 1972.

Elser, R. The social position of hearing handicapped children in regular grades. *Exceptional Children,* 1959, *25.* 305–309.

Evans, D. Experiential deprevation: unresolved factors in the impoverished socialization of deaf school children in residence. *American Annals of the Deaf,* 1975, *120,* 545–554.

Farrugia, C. A. S., & Austin, G. F. A study of social-emotional adjustment patterns of hearing-impaired students in different educational settings. *American Annals of the Deaf,* 1980, *125,* 535–541.

Gentile, A., & McCarthy, B. *Additional handicapping conditions among hearing impaired students. United States: 1971-1972* (Report Number 14, Series D). Washington, D.C.: Gallaudet College, Office of Demographic Studies, 1973.

Gonzales, R. Mainstreaming your hearing impaired child in 1980; still an oversimplification. *Journal of Research and Development in Education,* 1980, *4,* 15–21.

Jensema, C. The relationship between academic achievement and the demographic characteristics of hearing impaired children and youth (Report Number 2, Series R). Washington, D.C.: Gallaudet College, Office of Demographic Studies, 1975.

Karchmer, M., & Kirwin, L. The use of hearing aids by hearing impaired students in the United States (Report Number 2, Series S). Washington, D.C.: Gallaudet College, Office of Demographic Studies, 1977.

Karchmer, M., & Petersen, L. Commuter students at residential schools for the deaf. Washington, D.C.: Gallaudet College, Office of Demographic Studies, 1980.

Karchmer, M., & Trybus, R. Who are the deaf children in "Mainstream" programs? (Report Number 4, Series R). Washington, D.C.: Gallaudet College, Office of Demographic Studies, 1977.

Kennedy, P., Northcott, W. H., McCauley, R. W., & Williams, S. M. Longitudinal sociometric and cross-sectional data on mainstreaming hearing impaired children: implications for preschool programming. The Volta Review, 1976, 78, 71–81.

Klopping, J. W. E. Language understanding of deaf students under three auditory-visual stimulus conditions. American Annals of the Deaf, 1972, 117, 389–396.

Liben, L. S. The development of deaf children: an overview of issues. In L. S. Liben (Ed.), Deaf children: developmental perspectives. New York: Academic Press, 1978.

McConnell, R., & Liff, S. The rationale for early identification and intervention. Otolaryngologic Clinics of North America, 1975, 8, 77–87.

McGee, D. Mainstreaming problems and procedures: age 6-12. In G. Nix (Ed.), Mainstream education for hearing impaired children and youth. New York: Grune and Stratton, 1976.

McHugh, D. A view of deaf people in terms of Super's theory of vocational development. Journal of Rehabilitation of the Deaf, 1975, 9, 1–11.

Meadow, K. P. The "natural history" of a research project. In L. S. Liben (Ed.), Deaf children: developmental perspectives. New York: Academic Press, 1978.

Moores, D. F. Educating the deaf: psychology, principles and practices (2nd ed.). Boston: Houghton Mifflin, 1982.

Moores, D. F., Weiss, K. L., & Goodwin, M. W. Evaluation of programs for hearing impaired children: report of 1973–1974 (Research Report Number 81). Minneapolis: University of Minnesota, Research, Development, and Demonstration Center in Education of Handicapped Children, 1974.

Northcott, W. H. The hearing impaired child in a regular classroom: preschool, elementary, and secondary years. Washington, D.C.: Alexander Graham Bell Association for the Deaf, 1973.

O'Connor, D.C. The investigation of the deaf in schools for normally hearing. In I. S. Fusfeld (Ed.), A handbook of readings in education of the deaf and postschool implications. Springfield, Illinois: Charles C. Thomas, 1967.

Ously, J. C. A study of the relationships between accoustically handicapped children's academic achievement, their parents' attitudes, and other selected variables. (Doctoral dissertation, Greeley, University of Northern Colorado, 1973). Dissertation Abstracts International, 1974, 34, 4042A–4043A.

Pflaster, G. A factor analysis of variables related to academic performance of hearing impaired children in regular classes. The Volta Review, 1980, 82, 71–84.

Quigley, S., & Frisina, D. Institutionalization and psycheducational development of deaf children. Urbana, Illinois: Institute for Research on Exceptional Children, 1961.

Quigley, S. P., & Kretschmer, R. E. The education of deaf children. Baltimore: University Park Press, 1982.

Rawlings, B., & Trybus, R. Personnel, facilities and services available in schools and classes for hearing impaired children in the United States. American Annals of the Deaf Directory of Programs, 1978, 123, 99–114.

Reich, C., Hambleton, D., & Houldin, B. K. The integration of hearing impaired children in regular classrooms. *American Annals of the Deaf*, 1977, *122*, 534–543.

Ries, P. *Associations between achievement test performance and selected characteristics of hearing impaired students in special education programs: United States, Spring, 1971* (Report Number 13, Series D). Washington, D.C.: Gallaudet College, Office of Demographic Studies, 1973.

Rister, A. Deaf children in mainstream education. *The Volta Review*, 1975, *77*, 279–290.

Sarfaty, L., & Katz, S. The self-concept and adjustment patterns of hearing-impaired pupils in different school settings. *American Annals of the Deaf*, 1978, *123*, 438–441.

Shears, L. N., & Jensema, C. J. Social acceptability of anomalous persons. *Exceptional Children*, 1969, *36*, 91–96.

Shepard, N., Davis, J., Gorga, M., & Stelmachowicz, P. Characteristics of hearing-impaired children in the public schools. Part I. Demographic Data. *Journal of Speech and Hearing Disorder*, 1981, *46*, 123–129.

Teller, H. E., Jr. The relationship of parent attitudes with successful integration of hearing impaired children into regular classrooms (Doctoral dissertation, University of Alabama, 1974). *Dissertation Abstracts International*, 1975, *36*, 821A–822A.

Trybus, R. J., & Karchmer, M. A. School achievement status and growth patterns. *American Annals of the Deaf*, 1977, *122*, 62–69.

van den Horst, A. P. J. M. Defective hearing, school achievements, and school choice. *The Teacher of the Deaf*, 1971, *69*, 398–414.

Vernon, M., & Prickett, H. Mainstreaming, past and present: some issues and a model plan. *Audiology and Hearing Education*, 1976, *1&2*, 9–13.

## REFERENCE NOTES

1.  Karchmer, M., Trybus, R., & Paquin, M. *Early manual communication, parental hearing status, and the academic achievement of deaf students.* Paper presented at the American Education Research Association Annual Meeting, Toronto, Ontario, Canada, 1978.

*Charlene M. Kampfe*

# 7

# Mainstreaming: Some Practical Suggestions for Teachers and Administrators

Mainstreaming can be broadly defined as the placement of hearing-impaired students in classrooms and/or schools with normally hearing students. Providing this type of educational setting requires dedication, enthusiasm, and in-depth knowledge of the physical, psychosocial, and educational aspects of deafness. It also requires familiarity with methods of facilitating communication between hearing-impaired children and important other people in the school and community.

The purpose of this chapter is to provide the regular school teacher and administrator with some practical suggestions for providing an education to children with hearing impairments. It offers a good starting point for anyone desiring basic knowledge of the techniques of working with these children. Because of their importance, even the most logical suggestions have been included here.

## SUGGESTIONS FOR TEACHERS

Regular classroom teachers who are presently or about to serve hearing-impaired students can benefit from a few tips for working with this population. For easy reference, these suggestions are presented un-

THE HEARING-IMPAIRED CHILD IN SCHOOL
ISBN 0-8089-1663-7

der the subtopics of (1) physical environment, (2) communication, (3) classroom, and (4) professional development.

## Physical Environment

The design of the classroom is important to the success of the student who is hearing impaired. In preparing the classroom, three primary points should be kept in mind: (1) the child must be able to clearly see the face of the person who is talking; (2) the child should be near the person who is talking; and (3) the child must not be exposed to unnecessary noise.

The student's need to see the speaker's lips and facial expressions is vital. This is particularly true if sign language is not used. To facilitate this, the teacher should place the child's desk in positions that offer optimal viewing of all persons in the classroom. A semicircular seating arrangement is useful for this purpose. This arrangement can be effective for both large and small groups.

Perhaps even more important than a formal seating arrangement is flexibility in seating. The student should be allowed to exhange seats with other students as activities change (Birch, 1975; Gildston, 1973). Allowing the child to move to positions of optimal viewing will also give the teacher more flexibility in planning classroom activities. To avoid overemphasizing the child's hearing impairment, however, it is important that seating adjustments be done as unobtrusively as possible.

Lighting is important. The classroom should provide an unflickering light source that offers maximum output without glare. The light source should be on the face of the speaker and not in the eyes of the student. A common error is to stand in front of a light source (i.e., stand with one's back to a window). This creates a silhouette effect that results in extreme difficulty in seeing facial expressions or lip movements (Birch, 1975; Gildston, 1973).

Distance between the speaker and the child is also an important consideration. As the speaker moves away from the listener, the ability to hear and to understand speech decreases exponentially (Birch, 1975; Gildston, 1973). A general rule might be, "the closer the better"; however, 6 feet is optimal for speech reading.

Noise of any type interferes greatly with the ability to understand speech (Birch, 1975). This is especially true for children with certain types of hearing losses and for those wearing hearing aids (Stassen, 1973). Building noises, movement of chairs, group work that involves several people talking at one time, mechanical equipment such as fans and heaters, background music, buzzing lights, and classroom pet sounds will all interfere with speech discrimination.

Suggestions regarding noise levels in the classroom are as follows:

1.   Classroom surfaces such as walls, ceilings, floors, furniture, and windows should be covered with materials that absorb unnecessary noise. Examples of such materials are draperies, textured wallpaper or plaster, upholstery, carpeting, and acoustical tile. Hard, smooth surfaces should be avoided (Stassen 1973).

2.   Mechanical noises in the classroom should be minimized. Noisy equipment should be either removed or muffled by padding or oiling. It may be necessary to obtain the advice of a mechanical engineer regarding alterations that would decrease noises made by machines.

3.   It will be more difficult for the child to understand speech when the class is involved in group activities (Gildston, 1973). During these activities, special care should be taken to ensure that the child is not missing important messages.

4.   The classroom should not be situated near noisy areas such as gymnasiums, lunchrooms, or playgrounds.

5.   Hall noises can be avoided by selecting a classroom that is located away from heavy traffic areas. Since this is not always possible, the teacher can post notices and inform other personnel of the need for quiet halls outside the classroom.

6.   Hearing-impaired children should not be seated near sources of noise (i.e., halls, doors, outside windows, fans). This is especially critical for children who wear hearing aids.

7.   Class activities in large, echoing rooms such as gymnasiums and lunchrooms should be kept at a minimum, or at least controlled (Stassen, 1973).

## Communication

In addition to understanding the importance of proximity, lighting, and noise, the teacher needs to know how to communicate with the child and how to facilitate communication between others and the child. The following suggestions can apply to both teachers who use manual communication and those who do not.

ARTICULATE CLEARLY.   Increasing the loudness of the voice does not generally help the child's understanding. More important techniques are speaking at moderate speeds, enunciating clearly, and lowering the pitch (not the volume) of the voice. In using these techniques, never overemphasize mouth motions. These exaggerations will make speech reading more difficult (Birch, 1975; Gildston, 1973).

FACE THE HEARING-IMPAIRED STUDENT DIRECTLY.   It is much more difficult to speech read from the side than from directly ahead (Birch, 1975; Stassen, 1973).

DO NOT EAT, CHEW GUM, OR PLACE ANY OBJECT IN OR NEAR THE MOUTH WHEN SPEAKING.   Likewise, do not put your hands over your mouth or touch your face when communicating with the child.

USE FACIAL AND BODY EXPRESSIONS.   These perform a similar function as tone of voice. Since the hearing-impaired child may be unable to obtain clues from differences in tone, these clues must come from the face and body of the speaker. Speech reading is much easier when these expressions "match" the conversation (Berger, 1982). Without them, the child may understand the words spoken, but may misinterpret their meaning.

KEEP HAIR STYLES AWAY FROM THE FACE.   Long hair and beards often hide important facial clues and mouth movements for speech reading.

AVOID MOVING AROUND THE ROOM WHILE SPEAKING.   This makes speech reading difficult (Gildston, 1973).

KEEP YOUR FACE CLEAR.   Do not look down at books or notes and/or hold them in front of your face when reading aloud (Birch, 1975; Gildston, 1973).

SPEAK ONLY WHEN FACING THE CLASS.   When writing on the chalkboard, do not speak until you have finished writing and can face the class (Birch, 1975; Gildston, 1973).

GIVE CLUES.   Situational clues regarding the topic of conversation are important in speech reading and in the use of residual hearing. Following are some ways to provide these clues:

- If you do not use manual communication, natural gestures should be used. These gestures should not be exaggerated. Simple, normal use of hands and body are preferable. These can include pointing to an object, walking toward it, glancing at it, or touching it (Birch, 1975; Berger, 1972; Stassen, 1973).
- Use pictures and other visual aids to provide clues and/or to clarify points (Birch, 1975; Gildston, 1973; Stassen, 1973).
- Write important phrases or words on the chalkboard. This will inform the student of the topic of conversation and will lessen the likelihood that major points will be missed (Birch, 1975; Gildston, 1973; Northcott, 1973; Stassen, 1973). When using the chalkboard, repeat the written statements verbally. This will give the student

the opportunity to associate your lip movements with the words and phrases you will be using in the lecture.

• Another method of familiarizing the student with important terms is to ask the parents to discuss them with their child before the lecture. Seeing and hearing the vocabulary in advance will help the individual follow the lecture (Gildston, 1973).

• In class discussions, look at the students who are speaking. Gestures made toward these persons will also give the hearing-impaired child a clue as to where to look (Stassen, 1973).

BE SURE MAJOR POINTS ARE UNDERSTOOD.    Remember that the child cannot see your face when taking notes or doing assignments. When lecturing, observe the student to be sure that major points are being received. Since waiting for the child to look up can interfere with smooth presentations, alternatives include supplying a copy of the lecture notes and/or making arrangements with normally hearing students to share notes with the child (Birch, 1975).

BE AWARE OF COLDS OR ALLERGIES.    These can temporarily reduce the student's ability to hear (Gildston, 1973).

WATCH FOR SIGNALS OF CONFUSION.    Be alert to any signs of misunderstanding or failure to receive a message. A slow positive head shake or a blank stare from the child may be a signal that the statement has not been received or understood (Birch, 1975).

Following are some suggestions that will help the students in these situations:

• The child should be encouraged to ask for repeats when messages are not received or understood (Gildston, 1973).

• If the child is embarrassed about asking continually for repeats, subtle signals can be arranged to inform you of this need.

• If the child appears not to understand, discretely ask him or her to repeat what has been said or to answer a question regarding the topic (Birch, 1975).

• If the child does not understand something the first time, rephrase the sentence (Birch, 1975). A rephrased statement may be easier to speech read and/or to hear than the original statement.

• When asked to repeat something, do not use single words. These are more difficult to speech read than phrases (Birch, 1975; Gildston, 1973).

WATCH THE POSITION OF A CHILD WEARING A HEARING AID.    The child who wears a hearing aid should be seated in positions that will allow maximum use of that aid (Northcott, 1975). For example, if an aid is worn on the left ear, the child's left ear should not face the wall.

HAVE SOME LIGHT AVAILABLE WHEN SHOWING FILMS.   When showing films that you plan to make oral comments on, be certain that the child is able to see your face. This can be done by keeping a light on or by opening a window curtain.

## Classroom

Other tips that might be helpful in the classroom are as follows.

TEACH-RETEACH METHOD.   Many regular classroom teachers have found the teach-reteach method to be helpful especially with regard to teaching communication skills, language skills, subjects with high verbal content, and subjects required for graduation. Special education teachers, itinerant teachers, and resource room teachers can be of great benefit when using this method (Brill, 1978).

SPEECH AND AUDITORY TRAINING.   Request regular speech and auditory training for the child. These should be provided by qualified professionals.

SETTING GOALS.   Work closely with the special education teacher, resource room teacher, itinerant teacher, and speech therapist to ensure that similar goals have been set for the student (Birch, 1975).

CLASSROOM ACTIVITY SCHEDULES.   Avoid scheduling important classroom activities when the child is with specialists, such as the speech therapist or the itinerant teacher.

STUDENT ATTENTION SPAN.   Remember that speech reading and the use of residual hearing can be extremely tiring for the student (Courtman-Davies, 1979; Gildston, 1973). What may seem like boredom or disinterest may simply be a sign that the child is resting.

SOCIALIZATION.   Be alert to any problems the child might have with regard to socialization. Hearing-impaired students may feel overwhelmed when entering into a classroom with normally hearing students (Brill, 1978; Sussman, 1970). Unless they receive emotional support from the teacher and from other students, this problem may continue. Suggestions for counteracting this are listed below:

- Request an orientation program regarding hearing impairment for normally hearing students, secretaries, nurses, other teachers, and administrators (Brill, 1978).

• Describe the hearing aid and its function to normally hearing students. It is sometimes helpful to compare hearing aids to glasses. Although the two are quite different, the analogy might help to decrease some of the barriers between the hearing-impaired student and the other students in the school (Stassen, 1973).
• Request that normally hearing students be given credit for attending classes regarding hearing impairment (i.e., communication methods, psychosocial aspects) (Brill, 1978).
• Show that you respect the hearing-impaired child and see him or her as a person of worth. Hopefully, your attitude will be reflected by the attitudes of the normally hearing students in the classroom (Birch, 1975).

PARENTAL INVOLVEMENT.  Attempt to involve parents in the educational process. Elicit their help in teaching communication skills, in helping with homework, and in giving emotional support. This can be accomplished through a regular, organized program (Auble, 1973; Brill, 1978, Courtman-Davies, 1979).

Although parental involvement is extremely important, parents should not be forced to provide therapy or teaching. Neither should they be encouraged to spend most of their time with their child in a therapeutic or teaching role. In some cases, this type of involvement may interfere with normal interaction between siblings and parents and, therefore, may be more destructive than helpful.

READING LEVELS.  Be aware that many hearing-impaired children read at levels that are much lower than their normally hearing peers (Trybus & Karchmer, 1977). As a result, these students may have difficulty in classes that require high verbal ability and, therefore, may require special tutoring in these areas.

Hearing-impaired children are often misdiagnosed because the language and reading levels of tests for intelligence, aptitude, and personality are not appropriate for them. Because these tests may be measuring the student's language and reading skills rather than the characteristics they were intended to measure, it is generally advisable to question any low scores on verbal tests (Moores, 1982).

It has been speculated that low language and reading levels of hearing-impaired children are due, in part, to environmental conditions (i.e., lack of exposure to spoken or signed language). To counteract this, these children should be given every opportunity to communicate with others and to participate in language building exercises.

HEARING AIDS.  Encourage the child to use a hearing aid when one is prescribed. Ensure that the aid is functioning (Birch, 1975; Courtman-

Davies, 1979). A hearing aid is easily damaged by the activities of children. It can also be rendered useless because of failure to change batteries on a regular basis (at least every 4 to 8 days). To make certain that the aid is operational, it should be checked on a daily basis. Ideally, this should be done at home by the parents; however, to assure regularity and accuracy of the check, it should probably be done at the school. The check is simple to perform, requires minimal equipment, and can be conducted after a short training period (perhaps one to two hours). This check is described in Chapter 4.

Although the check may take only a few minutes, it can be an annoying additional task during the morning preparation for class. For this reason, the school nurse, rather than the teacher, should be responsible for this duty.

SPEECH.    Encourage the child to use speech and to be involved in oral communication in the classroom (Brill, 1978).

MANUAL COMMUNICATION.    Use sign language and/or an interpreter if the student's primary method of communication is manual communication. Although it is preferable to sign for yourself, if this is not possible, an interpreter can provide a valuable link between you and the child. The interpreter can also be used when the child is interacting with other students or other personnel.

Persons who have never worked with interpreters are often confused about their roles. Basically, these professionals should be thought of as the ears and, if applicable, the voice of the student. However, some function as tutors as well (Gonzales, 1980). Additional information regarding the use of interpreters can be found in Chapter 14.

Be wary of your own or other professionals' biases regarding the issues of mainstreaming versus segregation and/or total communication versus the oral method. Do not accept other professionals' points of view until you have fully considered both sides of each of these issues. It is best to remember that, although many people feel strongly about one or the other, there is little conclusive evidence that one method or program setting is better than another.

Do not force parents to choose the method of communication or the educational setting for their child based on your opinion. It is better to inform them of the benefits and limitations of the various options and to allow them to make their own decisions based on objective information (Courtman-Davies, 1979).

THE STUDENT AS AN INDIVIDUAL.    Do not expect that all hearing-impaired children will be affected in the same way by their hearing losses (Gildston, 1973). Always think of the student as an individual and not as a person who fits into a category called "hearing impaired," with characteristics like all others with this disability.

EXPECTATIONS.  Despite the child's need for certain special services and communication considerations, expect the same behavior, responsibility, and effort from this student as expected from the normally hearing students in the class (Birch, 1975; Brill, 1978; Gildston, 1973). It does not help the student to have lower or higher expectations of him or her than other students in the class.

## Professional Development

It is vital that the teacher have knowledge and understanding of hearing impairment and its effects on students. The following is a list of suggestions for obtaining this information.

REQUEST INSERVICE TRAINING.  There should be inservice training both before the hearing-impaired child enters the classroom and on a continuing basis (Brill, 1978). This training should include, but not be limited to:

- different types of hearing losses and their possible effects on the student
- different types of hearing aids—their benefits and limitations
- care of hearing aids
- psychosocial aspects of deafness
- techniques for improving communication between the teacher and student
- teaching methods related to communication skills and other important academic areas
- manual communication

GET ADVICE FROM A SPECIALIST.  Ask the special education teacher, supervisor, or audiologist for advice regarding the type of loss the child has and what its effect might be. Remember that there are many different types of hearing losses, and that each can affect the hearing-impaired child differently. Remember also that similar hearing losses do not always produce the same results.

OBSERVE.  Request observations of special education teachers as they work with hearing-impaired students (Birch, 1975).

TAKE A COURSE.  Request permission to enroll in classes related to hearing impairment. School districts sometimes offer reimbursement to teachers who attend job-related college courses.

OBTAIN READING MATERIALS.   Many books and articles offer both practical advice and theoretical background for working with persons who have a hearing impairment.

## SUGGESTIONS FOR ADMINISTRATORS

Administrative decisions regarding mainstreaming of students with hearing impairments must be based on complete information regarding this disability. Since many administrators do not have the time to obtain this information, the following list has been prepared to offer some of the basic points that should be considered with regard to offering an integrated education to these students. This list includes information regarding special service needs, physical plant accommodations, staffing requirements, and other items related to serving children with hearing impairments.

Although this list has been prepared for administrators who have not yet begun to offer mainstreaming to hearing-impaired children, it can also be used by principals and superintendents whose schools are already serving this group.

SUPPORT FOR THE PROGRAM.   Before starting a mainstreamed program, the administrator should obtain assurance that the school board and community are committed to integration. This commitment will improve the chances for success and enhance continued funding (Birch, 1975).

CONSULTATION.   Administrators of other integrated programs of similar sized schools should be consulted. It is expected that these persons will be able to provide information regarding the limitations and benefits of such programs and to offer suggestions for beginning or improving services for the hearing impaired.

OPTIONS.   Not all hearing-impaired children will benefit from the same type of educational setting. Because it is important to meet the individual needs of each child, the school should be prepared to provide a wide range of options, which include itinerant teachers, resource rooms, special classes, and team teaching (Brill, 1978; Moores, 1982). These and other options are described in Chapter 6 of this book.

Both total communication and an oral approach to teaching should be available (Brill, 1978). These approaches are described in Chapters 6 and 10 of this book.

The entire school enrollment should be considered. Brill (1978) suggests that school districts with total enrollments of less than 100,000 students will probably not have large enough hearing-impaired populations to provide a full range of options to these children. There are, however, schools with student populations of 10,000 who offer excellent programs for hearing-impaired children.

CRITERIA.    Criteria should be set for acceptance into the mainstreaming program. This criteria should be based on the characteristics of students who typically succeed in this type of setting (Brill, 1978; Courtman-Davies, 1979). Chapter 6 of this book describes the major criteria that should be considered.

ENVIRONMENT.    An appropriate physical environment should be provided:

- Warning signals should be visual (Birch, 1975).
- Announcements should be printed or conveyed visually.
- Classrooms should be located away from noisy building areas (i.e., busy halls, gymnasiums, eating areas, play areas).
- The noise from heating and cooling systems should be kept at a minimum.
- Classrooms should be furnished with noise absorbing materials (i.e., draperies, acoustical tile, carpeting, upholstery, textured walls and ceilings).
- Mechanical engineers should be consulted regarding reduction of noise in the classroom.

EXPERIENCED TEACHERS.    Teachers should be selected on the basis of past performance and special skills in working with disabled children. Those with training or experience in working with hearing-impaired children are preferable.

Only teachers who are willing and highly motivated to instruct children with hearing impairments should be selected. A teacher who is unwilling to serve this population should never be forced to do so (Auble, 1973; Birch, 1975).

SUPPORT FOR THE TEACHERS.    Once selected, teachers should be given support by the administration (Auble, 1973; Birch, 1975):

- The teacher should receive in-depth orientation to deafness before attempting to serve a hearing-impaired child in the regular classroom (Birch, 1975; Brill, 1978).
- Supervision, consultation, and inservice training should be available on a continuing basis (Birch, 1975; Brill, 1978).
- The number of students in the classroom should be decreased as the number of hearing-impaired students is increased (Auble, 1973).

- Interpreters should be provided for children whose primary method of communication is sign language (Brill, 1978).
- School personnel (i.e., secretaries, librarians, physical education teachers) who will be working with the students should receive an orientation to hearing impairment (Brill, 1978).
- An individual should be assigned to conduct a daily hearing aid check—this duty might best be performed by the school nurse.
- Provision should be made for complete, valid evaluations of each child's hearing loss. The implications of these losses should be carefully explained to the teacher (Brill, 1978). These evaluations should be conducted by an audiologist; not by a school nurse or hearing aid dealer.
- School psychologists should have knowledge of the impact of a hearing impairment and should be able to communicate with children who have this disability (Brill, 1978). They should know the *limitations* of the tests they are using and how these instruments should be interpreted in relation to hearing impairment.
- School counselors should be familiar with the psychosocial aspects of hearing impairment and should be able to communicate with students with this disability.
- Speech-language therapists and/or other speech clinicians should be scheduled on a regular basis. These persons should provide direct speech, speech reading, and auditory training to the child as well as consultation to the teacher (Northcott, 1973).
- Notetakers should be provided to assure that the student is receiving all pertinent information (Brill, 1974).
- Itinerant teachers, resource rooms, and special education teachers should be available for tutoring in verbal subject areas and in subjects required for graduation (Brill, 1978).

ORIENTATION.   Orientation to hearing impairment should be scheduled for students who will share the classroom with the hearing-impaired child. This orientation should also be made available to other students of the school (Brill, 1978).

Classes for credit regarding communication methods and physical and psychosocial aspects of deafness can be offered to the student body (Brill, 1978).

PROGRAM FOR THE PARENTS.   An organized program for parents is extremely helpful in eliciting their support. Such a program should also help the parents learn more about their children's hearing impairments and their own feelings about these disabilities (Auble, 1973; Brill, 1978).

COUNSELING.   Family counseling should be made available to parents of hearing-impaired children (Luterman, 1979).

MODELS FOR THE STUDENTS.   Hearing-impaired adults should be hired or invited into the school to provide models for the hearing-impaired students (Brill, 1978).

MODEL FOR THE COMMUNITY AND TEACHERS.   Throughout the planning and implementation process, the administrator should provide a positive model regarding commitment to the program (Birch, 1975).

## SUMMARY

Unless the teacher and administrator have in-depth knowledge of hearing impairment, mainstreamed programs will be nothing more than placement of hearing-impaired students into regular classrooms or schools without meeting these children's special needs.

The suggestions presented in this chapter are considered basic. Teachers and administrators are encouraged to seek further information before attempting to serve students with this disability in their regular schools. This book has been designed to provide this information. Other excellent materials can be found in the reference section of this chapter.

## REFERENCES

Auble, L.F. The integrated superintendent: normalization can be a reality. In W.H. Northcott (Ed.), *The hearing impaired child in a regular classroom: preschool, elementary and secondary years. A guide for the classroom teacher/administrator.* Washington, D.C.: Alexander Graham Bell Association for the Deaf, 1973.

Berger, K.W. *Speechreading principles and methods.* Baltimore: National Educational Press, 1972.

Birch, J. W. *Hearing impaired children in the mainstream.* St. Paul: Leadership Training Institute/Special Education, University of Minnesota, 1975.

Brill, R.G. *The education of the deaf: administrative and professional developments.* Washington, D.C.: Gallaudet College Press, 1974.

Brill, R.G. *Mainstreaming the prelingually deaf child.* Washington, D.C.: Gallaudet College Press, 1978.

Courtman-Davis, M. *Your deaf child's speech and language.* London: The Bodley Head Ltd., 1979.

Gonzales, R. Mainstreaming your hearing impaired child in 1980: still an oversimplification. *Journal of Research and Development in Education,* 1980, 4, 19–21.

Gildston, P. The hearing impaired child in the classroom: a guide for the classroom teacher. In W.H. Northcott (Ed.), *The hearing impaired child in a regular classroom: preschool, elementary, and secondary years. A guide for the classroom teacher/administrator.* Washington D.C.: Alexander Graham Bell Association for the Deaf, Inc., 1973.

Luterman, D. *Counseling parents of hearing impaired children.* Boston: Little, Brown, & Co., 1979.

Moores, D.F. *Educating the deaf: psychology, principles and practices* (2nd ed.). Boston: Houghton-Mifflin, 1982.

Northcott, W.H. A speech clinician as multidisciplinary team member. In W.H. Northcott (Ed.), *The hearing impaired child in a regular classroom: preschool, elementary, and secondary years. A guide for the classroom teacher/administrator.* Washington, D.C.: Alexander Graham Bell Association for the Deaf, 1973.

Stassen, R.A. I have one in my class who's wearing hearing aids! In W.H. Northcott (Ed.), *The hearing impaired child in a regular classroom: preschool, elementary, and secondary years. A guide for the classroom teacher/administrator.* Washington, D.C.: Alexander Graham Bell Association for the Deaf, 1973.

Sussman, A.E. The comprehensive counseling needs of deaf persons. *Hearing and Speech News,* 1970, *38,* 12–13, 22,24.

Trybus, R.J., & Karchmer, M.A. School achievement status and growth patterns. *American Annals of the Deaf,* 1977, *122,* 62–69.

*Joyce Best,*
*Andrew Nielsen*

# 8

# The Development of Hearing-Impaired Children: The Relationship Between Home and School

The key to the maximum realization of a hearing-impaired child's potential is his or her accessibility to society's communication system. Just as stairs can make a building inaccessible to the physically disabled individual in a wheelchair, the lack of accessible language/communication makes the world of family, friends, and social and educational relationships with other people inaccessible to the hearing-impaired child.

No disability is more difficult for parents to comprehend than a hearing impairment. The handicap of a severe hearing disorder on a child's development of language, emotional development, and social development is generally beyond a parent's understanding. It is an invisible impairment; that is, it cannot be seen outwardly, making its impact even more bewildering for parents and teachers. The professional who first contacts the parents of a hearing-impaired child must remember that the parents may have received little or no counseling as to the nature of their child's disability. If parents receive the proper counseling and are educated as to their child's special needs, their support can be invaluable in the development of language and in the child's social and emotional development.

This chapter will present information on the impact a hearing loss has upon the family unit, and what may be done through the inter-relationship of that unit and the school to enhance the hearing-impaired child's development. The importance of communication in the family unit and activities to develop the hearing-impaired child's communication skills are discussed. Other areas presented include sex education, discipline, values development, and other issues pertinent to the development of hearing-impaired children.

A hearing impairment represents more than the loss of one individual's ability to detect physical sound. It has an impact on the total family unit. A hearing impairment represents a social-cognitive barrier to the individual. A total family commitment is required to help the hearing-impaired individual free himself or herself from the restraints of this barrier. To the family this means modifying social situations so family members can include the hearing-disabled individual.

## THE IMPORTANCE OF LANGUAGE

What does it mean to parents to have a hearing-impaired youngster? Here are some relevant facts that may aid parents in grasping the impact of a hearing impairment.

1.  Ninety-five percent of a child's native language is acquired through the auditory channel.
2.  The average normally hearing child entering school at age 5 will have a receptive vocabulary of six to ten thousand words.
3.  By age 4 the typical hearing child will be using 90 percent of the grammatical concepts of the English language correctly.
4.  The vocabulary and grammatical concepts will have been learned through interaction with the family unit and others in the child's immediate environment.

Language is the natural spoken and written, heard and read symbol system common to any given society (i.e., English, French, Spanish). Language enables one to communicate needs, wants, and all prior learned concepts (knowledge). Language affects one's intellectual processing through interaction with others, the speed with which our intellectual processes develop, and the rate at which one can problem-solve.

Left alone and not accommodated and assimilated into the family unit, the hearing-impaired individual has little chance at developing into a well-adjusted, confident individual. The key to ensuring a well-adjusted and developed individual is communication. A hearing impairment need not be a social-cognitive barrier if the family unit includes the hearing-impaired youngster within their communication circle.

Historically, the *school* has been seen as the "primary educator" for the hearing-impaired youngster. Unfortunately, educators have been all too willing to assume that role and responsibility. In too many instances parents also placed primary responsibility on the schools for educating their hearing-impaired children. Instead, education of the hearing-impaired child should be a joint venture between family and educator and/or the hearing specialist in the school.

## THE HOME—A PLACE FOR THE DEVELOPMENT OF LANGUAGE

The home is where the child spends the majority of his or her time. As an infant even into young adulthood, the home is the principal base of all social adventures. Communication, in whatever form, begins in the home. Communication is not limited to talking, signing, or writing. It is the interaction of the child and those in his or her immediate environment. The family unit—their thoughts, attitudes, and values—should be communicated to the child directly and indirectly in order for that child to grow in self-understanding. It is within this environment that the child's self-esteem, or lack of it, grows and is nurtured.

### Helping the Hearing-Impaired Child Develop A Sense of Self-Esteem

It is difficult to teach parenting, let alone parenting of a disabled child. How does a parent know what direction to take? Where to start? Whose answers to believe? The best response to these questions can be: "Listen to all that the educators say, evaluate what the specialists tell, but then, yes, you are the parents of an exceptional child. He or she is a part of you and your family . . . treat the child as a functioning contributing member of the family unit, not as an addition or burden, or someone who needs special privileges." The hearing-impaired child can perceive his acceptance, or the lack of it, by the way he is included in family life: arguments, jokes, or perhaps general discussions held at dinner time. If this inclusion is made, the child's hearing loss does not need to be a barrier to developing a healthy self-esteem.

Helping a child develop a healthy self-esteem is no easy task. Many strategies are necessary, since each family is unique in its needs and wants and in its approaches to fulfilling family members' needs. Family life, then, becomes a matter of choices. How each family makes those choices, and the criteria it uses in making choices, become its value system.

If parents desire to determine their values, they may examine how they spend their time and resources. If family and the security of each family member is valued, it will be reflected in the time a parent devotes to the family. Helping hearing-impaired children develop a positive self-esteem is not a one-time thing. It requires time and the support of the family and the educators who work with the child.

Once a family has made a commitment to help this child develop as a person who feels wanted, loved, and secure, they will have to develop other qualities. Two essential qualities that each family member must develop are (1) patience and (2) a sense of humor. Lastly, they must become familiar with the basic characteristics of child development. An excellent resource book for parents is *Child Behavior from Birth to Ten* by Ilg and Ames.

A family must give the child a feeling of acceptance by including him in family communication and allowing the experience of life's ups and downs. Family members must remember that a hearing-impaired child is a child first. They should view the hearing-impaired child as a child with a hearing disability, not a hearing disabled child.

The parents and educators of a hearing-impaired child must be alert for the potential development of two damaging attitudes: (1) self-pity and (2) overly self-critical. These attitudes are easily detectable if the parent and teacher "listen" to what the child is saying. The development of these attitudes may cripple the hearing-impaired child in the development of his or her full potential.

## Teaching the Child To Compensate

Through consistent communication with the hearing-impaired child, the parent must teach the child to compensate for the hearing deficit. The parent and teacher must help the child recognize his or her strengths and weaknesses. It is important that the hearing-impaired child develop a realistic view of his or her capabilities and how to compensate for the hearing deficit.

A child with a hearing deficit will have a positive self-esteem if the following points are kept in mind:

1. Parents should make a time commitment to communicate with the child each day.
2. Parents need patience, a sense of humor, and a knowledge of normal child development.

3. Feelings of rejection and over-protection should not be allowed to develop in the family.
4. Feelings of self-pity and self-criticism should not be allowed to develop in the child.
5. The child should be seen as a child first and as having a hearing impairment second.

The commitment of *time* must be stressed in light of the difficult decisions the family will face. For example, if the hearing-impaired child is to succeed, learning communication skills will take time for the family, tutoring in school subjects will take time, even explaining a joke will take time. As a reward, the family will have a tremendous and exhilarating feeling of accomplishment. The family, especially parents, must keep their eyes on the final goal—a child who will develop to his or her fullest potential.

## COMMUNICATION SYSTEMS AT HOME AND AT SCHOOL

To have an enriched language environment in the home, the family will have to seek out the communication system that is most appropriate for their hearing-impaired family member. There are many different viewpoints on what system is the best. It must be pointed out that all communication systems have positive points as well as weaknesses. A communication system may include an oral-aural system utilizing amplification and speech reading skills, or it may include an oral-aural visual system utilizing amplification, speech reading, and a signing system. Today the major signing systems include the American Sign Language (ASL), Signed English, Signing Exact English, Seeing Essential English, the Rochester Method (finger spelling), and a system that emphasizes speech development utilizing visual cues, which is called Cued Speech. Professionals in the educational treatment of hearing-impaired students recognize that each system is only as good as the support it gets in the home.

Some factors the professional service provider and the family will want to consider in selecting the appropriate system are:

1. extent of the hearing disability
2. other major physical or mental disabilities
3. age of onset of the hearing loss
4. age at time of identification of the hearing loss
5. proximity of educational facilities
6. willingness of the family to consider to relocate or to be closer to an appropriate educational facility.

It is the responsibility of the educational service provider to provide the parents with some knowledge of the wide range of communication systems available. The key in making the decision regarding the communication system is *how well does the system meet the total needs of the child.* This decision will probably be the most difficult one that a parent will have to make.

If the communication system that has been decided upon includes a form of manual communication, it is the responsibility of the parents to learn it as soon as possible and to keep their proficiency ahead of their child's skills so that language development can continue at home. If the parent and family members do not keep up with their child's skills, it will severely retard the child's language growth. If an oral-aural mode is the one to be stressed, the parents must also work closely with hearing specialists to develop a strong home language stimulation program.

## KNOWLEDGE OF CHILD DEVELOPMENT

A second requirement for parents of hearing-impaired children is that they learn the basic principles of child development and cognitive development. If the child's educational service provider will provide the parents with an opportunity to become familiar with these principles, it will alleviate many fears and apprehensions about their hearing-impaired child's development. The work at the Gesell Institute of Child Development, and the work of Swiss psychologist, Jean Piaget, offer invaluable tools for the hearing-impaired educational service provider and the parents of the children with hearing impairments.

## INDIRECT COMMUNICATION

A third requirement for parents of hearing-impaired children is that they realize the value of indirect communication. In too many families of hearing-impaired children only direct/directed communication is utilized. One must realize the tremendous amount of information the hearing person acquires by being a listener in conversations that do not directly involve him or her. A second concept involved in this indirect communication is motivation for growth so that the individual may become an active participant in such conversations. It will encourage the hearing-impaired individual to grow and develop language skills.

## FAMILY ISSUES

The child's language level will have a direct impact on many family issues. In the remainder of this chapter, four areas that most often arise in the parenting process will be addressed. The authors will discuss why communication is so relevant to the resolution of these issues, which include (1) discipline, (2) relationships, and (3) value systems.

## Discipline

An area many parents of handicapped children either inadvertently or purposely choose to avoid is that of discipline. There are no hard and fast rules in this area, whether or not a child is handicapped, but if he or she is going to develop as a socially and emotionally healthy child, consistent rules of discipline must be applied. A child who is underdisciplined will frequently show signs of desiring to be corrected. An undisciplined child will feel unwanted, even when the family says they love him or her. Actions often speak louder than words in this case. The child who has a high self-esteem is one who is loved, appreciated, and appropriately disciplined. He or she usually comes from a home that is more strict in discipline and is characterized by boundaries that were established early. To discipline does not necessarily mean the physical handling of the child. It should mean the drawing of guidelines—having rules and then sticking to them. The consequence for disobeying can range from isolation in a bedroom, sitting on a chair for a given period of time, or removal of a favorite activity for a specified period of time.

A child, whether hearing impaired or normally hearing, must be taught to know right and wrong, acceptable and unacceptable behaviors, in order to become an acceptable member in the family and the community. Guidelines should be established early, and consequences should be explained. Carry through cannot be over-emphasized. A family must outline what their needs and expectations are, and then develop their approach to making their child aware of them. The same approach should occur in the classroom or therapy session. Then, a child may misbehave because he or she does not understand the rule, or the child may be defiant because he or she decides to test the consequence.

## Relationships

THE MOTHER. The family is the root of a child's development. Although it is not the case in every family, it is often the mother who is the child's primary mentor. She is usually the first to discover that the child is having difficulty, taking the child to a doctor and then hearing specialist, and relating frustrations at her lack of understanding of unfamiliar terms and expectations. The infant and young child spend much time with mother. The child can perceive the tension each encounter brings on the road to the discovery of the hearing loss. If this continues at great lengths it is easy to understand how a child with minimal or no language skills may see him or herself as a misfit or a burden. Family arguments may be interpreted by the hearing-impaired child as the result of his or her handicap.

Mothers who spend a majority of time with their hearing-impaired children begin to "read" their wants and needs. At times an informal form of manual communication develops between mother and child. It is mother who first becomes involved in learning to communicate with the child. Each of these steps makes the child more dependent on her for information. The child's bond to mother becomes so strong the child may have difficulty developing a relationship with other family members. This dependence may cause family strain as other members vie for mother's attention.

If the attachment of the hearing-impaired child to mother is not evenly balanced with others, his or her socialization with peers and siblings will be limited, resulting in further isolation. A hearing-impaired child needs role models that others of similar age can provide. Without them the child's social-emotional skills will be diminished. This isolation can also result in the lack of other skills needed for cognitive growth, fine and gross motor skills, and the initiative to participate in activities that are new and different.

THE FATHER.   During the early stages of development, the father of the hearing-impaired child unfortunately may have been seen as only a shadow rather than a force in the development of his child. Relationships are too often hinged on mom "interpreting" what is said from one to the other. That interference of direct communication can lead to a distorted view and understanding of the father's role in the family. Even when dad takes manual communication classes, in the case of a profoundly hearing-impaired child, his skills may be less proficient than his wife's, and he becomes a victim of a child's impatience while he labors to tell the child about his day or explain a sporting event.

Providing a child a well-balanced input from the family is not an easy task. It is essential, however, that a balance be attempted. A child benefits from getting as much information as possible. He or she needs to be shown the processes in decision-making, consequences for those decisions, and how to deal with the outcomes. The child needs both male and female views on situations. It is not the educational institution's goal to teach values of the home. That should be a goal of the family.

A child can develop social and emotional behaviors with direction from the home. He or she needs to be told what is acceptable or not acceptable behavior. The child needs to know limits that are established and how they apply to the family members. The social and emotional well-being of the child cannot be assumed.

SIBLINGS.   The siblings also have a role to perform in the development of a hearing-impaired child. The brother(s) or sister(s) can be a hearing helper when they all play, or a defender when others criticize, developing a strong relationship between sibling(s) and hearing-impaired child that can be a critical element in how the child develops his or her ability to relate and interact with peers.

Jealousy is a factor that exists naturally and can develop into a barrier between normally hearing children and their hearing-impaired sibling. Parents must be conscious of the type and degree of treatment given and try to deal with it equally, or at least diplomatically, not making excuses for the "special" child. Special needs may be necessary and can be explained, but special treatment causes strain not only on the child-to-child relationships, but on the parent-to-child relationships as well.

## The Single Parent of A Hearing-Impaired Child

There is an apparent lack of information on single parents and their relationship in the social-emotional development of the hearing-impaired child. It seems logical that the single parent, for example, must work harder to develop skills that will facilitate communication between child and parent. Playing a dual role is difficult with normal children. Complicate the situation with a handicap, and it becomes an ever larger task. However, most single parents accept the challenge. Problems arise as the parent tries to establish new relationships with others. Often the hearing-impaired child dislikes sharing that parent with another adult.

Since a single parent may have limited time to spend with his or her child, that time needs to become quality time. As with the family unit, time shared can cause the child to develop either a sense of worth or isolation depending on the parent's approach.

There are no answers or cures for relationships between family and hearing-impaired child. An alert educator or specialist can aid when difficulties arise. Counseling and alternatives may be recommended. It is evident that the hearing-impaired child's ability to communicate his feelings in an open, honest, and accurate way assumes a close relationship with his or her family.

## A VALUE SYSTEM—THE BASIS FOR DECISION MAKING

Perhaps the greatest challenge facing the school and the home today is that of instilling a sound value system in children. Today's hearing-impaired adolescent is entering into a world filled with contradictions.

As one watches the news on television or reads the newspapers, the issues of society, including sexual freedom, homosexuality, drugs, alcohol, abortion, money, materialism, and others, are difficult to comprehend for the normally hearing adult who possesses normal language function, let alone a deaf adolescent.

What is a parent of the hearing-impaired child to do? What about the role of the school? Let us examine the limitations of the role of the school. For example, the school can realistically teach the student about the human body, awareness of emotions, and other such information. But can the school teach morality? Usually the answer is no because of the nature of its population. Within one classroom there is a variety of students from various backgrounds, all having their own beliefs and teachings regarding a given moral issue. The school can help the student understand how the body works, but not when to employ it. The teacher can help clarify values, but cannot develop them.

The hearing-impaired child will develop a value system. The nature of that value system will largely depend upon his or her environment outside of the school. It will probably be developed primarily by what the child experiences in the home. Once again the answer to this issue is *communication*. The parent, mother and father, must be able to communicate with their child. The hearing-impaired child must be able to experience indirect communication as the value systems are employed *by* the family *in* the family decision-making process. The parent must never risk endangering communication by reacting negatively to an adolescent's sometimes inappropriate questions.

One of the greatest experiences a parent and adolescent can have is taking a weekend vacation together. It can bring them together as no time at home can. Discussion times ensue of a personal family nature that may never have developed at home. On this "vacation," a father and son, or mother and daughter, can share feelings, answer questions, and explore relationships. Once the child has experienced this intimate time with the parent, he or she may feel much more at ease in approaching the parent with difficult questions.

## SUMMARY

If a hearing-impaired child is to realize his or her full intellectual potential, the child must be an active participant in the communication network in the home. A normal child will acquire language in two modes: he or she will grow as a result of direct communication; a greater growth, or motivation for growth, may be through indirect communication. As discussed earlier, indirect communication is one in which the hearing-impaired youngster is a passive-active observer. It is in this mode that the natural motivation to grow lingually-linguistically will be encouraged.

One of the most frequent criticisms leveled at the hearing-impaired child or adolescent is that he does not use "common sense." The reasons "common sense" may not develop is that there may be a reduction of direct communication in the life of a hearing-impaired youngster. If the child is not exposed to the language that goes with everyday experiences, his or her acquisition of knowledge on which to base decision making will be lacking. It must be emphasized that when a commitment is made to keep a severely hearing-impaired child in the home versus a residential placement, the family unit is making a decision that is going to be time consuming, and will also impact upon the family unit's relationship. It should also be mentioned, however, that these will be positive changes, changes that will draw the family together, changes that will give that family a sense of pride, and above all, can correctly bring home the real meaning of love in the family.

## SUGGESTED READINGS

Dobson, J. *Dare to discipline.* Wheaton, Illinois: Tyndale House Publishers, 1970.

Dobson, J. *Hide or seek.* Old Tappan, New Jersey: Fleming H. Revell, 1974.

Freeman, R., Carbin, C., & Boese, R. *Can't your child hear?* Baltimore: University Park Press, 1981.

Furth, H. *Piaget for teachers.* Englewood Cliffs, New Jersey: Prentice-Hall, 1970.

Gesell, A., & Ilg, F. *The child from five to ten.* New York & London: Harper & Brothers, 1946.

Ilg, F., & Ames, L. *Child behavior from birth to ten.* New York: Perennial Library, Harper & Row, 1955.

Singer, D., & Revenson, T. *A Piaget primer—how a child thinks.* New York: International Universities Press, 1978.

Ward, T. *Values begin at home.* Wheaton, Illinois: Victor Books, 1979.

## Appendix 8–1.  *Questions Most Often Asked by Parents of Hearing-Impaired Children*

Q.  What are things parents can do at home to aid in their child's language development?

A.  Parents should plan to spend quality time communicating with their child. With the young hearing-impaired child, this time is usually spent building vocabulary through action stories, naming things in their environment, and venturing out into the real world. As more vocabulary is gained, the parents can work with the child to express his thoughts and feelings. Parents and teachers must always be proper language models. Once a child is 6 or 7, keeping in mind his or her intellectual development, parents can begin to ask more questions and aid in the sharing of knowledge to help seek answers. School and home need to keep in constant contact to reinforce the learning that is taking place in both environments.

Q.  How does a parent keep communication channels open in adolescence?

A.  A hearing impairment, of course, does not eliminate or stop a child from entering this time in one's life. All children go through similar emotional stages in adolescence-rebellion, emotional highs and lows, and self-doubt. A parent can share some of their own intimate adolescent experiences, thus helping the child realize that these are natural happenings. A parent's answers to an adolescent's questions must be open and honest. If the situation becomes uncomfortable, the parents can ask for help from others (professionals) to discuss "touchy" subject areas with the child. This sharing is a continuing growth process for both parent and child that should have begun long before adolescence.

Q.  How do you talk to a hearing-impaired child about sex?

A.  First, parents or teachers need to be aware of when the child is ready to talk (i.e., first dance, bodily development, use of deodorant, etc.). When these changes begin to take place, the child is usually ready to seek out reasons to why things are occurring. The environment in which some of these conversations take place is important. A father may take his son for a walk or on a camping trip. A mother may talk while they are doing household activities or having lunch together. A word of caution is given to parents: do not be shocked by the way some questions are phrased. A hearing-impaired child with limited vocabulary regarding sexual information may use gestures or slang terms during questions that may take a parent back somewhat.

Q. *How can a parent teach a child responsibilities in the home?*

A. A parent must give the deaf child a chance to have assigned tasks within the home. This can be as simple as caring for his or her hearing aid, to picking up toys and helping to set the table. When the assigned responsibilities are not performed, the child must learn what the consequences are for lack of performance. Even if the consequences are discussed beforehand, enforcing them the first time will help the child understand how important it is to be responsible for his or her actions. In this regard, as in most others, a hearing-impaired child must be treated no differently than a normally hearing child. Responsibilities are responsibilities.

Q. *How does one not make the hearing-impaired child "special" in treatment when compared to others?*

A. Because of the attention demanded by a hearing-impaired child, this is difficult to do. The child should be given no more or less attention than other family members or students in the classroom. The hearing-impaired child needs to be treated equally. Rules should apply no differently unless circumstances warrant.

Q. *What is the father's role in raising the hearing-impaired child?*

A. Too often the father takes a back seat in raising a child with a hearing impairment. Out of default, he may find it easier to nod when he doesn't understand and to stay late at work. As the child becomes older, he or she may begin to see this as neglect and could resent the father for it. Even the father may not realize that it is from himself that a child develops a value system. The hearing-impaired child watches how the father makes decisions, his response to problem-solving, and his response to members of the family. The father must be assertive enough to be an "equal partner" in raising the child. He cannot afford to sit back and wait for the right moment if he wants to be a positive force with the child.

Q. *How can parents get extended family members—friends—to support discipline established in the home?*

A. It is important that discipline be consistent. As educators, we stress that concept to parents on a continuing basis. It must become their responsibility to make others aware in regard to how to react to certain behaviors their child may display. The parents initiative to carry through on established rules aids the child in acknowledging limits and becoming a socially acceptable member of the community.

Q. *How far should parents involve themselves in school decisions?*

A. A partnership should exist between home and school. Each needs to keep in constant contact with the other so there are no surprises on decisions made. Both must ask questions of the other. Defensiveness in responses must be avoided. This can result in a break in the communication process as well as a decline in effectiveness in dealing with a child who relys on the support of each.

Q.  *How does a child with a hearing loss develop a positive self-image when he learns he is different?*

A.  A positive self-image is the result of people in the child's environment who help him or her learn to compensate for the loss, and who steer the child into areas where success will be experienced.

Q.  *How far should a child be encouraged to participate in extracurricular activities?*

A.  Each hearing-impaired child should be encouraged to participate in activities where he or she may be the only student with a hearing loss. If it is a special club, sporting activity, or gathering that the child has interest in, he or she should be allowed to stay after school to participate. However, it is the parent's responsibility to not allow the child to quit the activity after one bad experience or because they didn't "make the first team." The child must learn that he or she has a responsibility to meet an obligation that was assumed when joining a club or sport.

Q.  *What does a specialist/educator tell a parent who appears to be over protective of their hearing-impaired child?*

A.  This situation is a normal response by parents when they have a child who has special needs. The long-range effects of over protectiveness needs to be pointed out. A negative impact on the child's emotional state is one possible result. The life of the family may then become dominated by the hearing-impaired child. The child may not grow socially or emotionally to adjust to the environment outside the home. Frustrations, confusions, fights, and limited contact may cause the family to resent the child. It is imperative that parents and other family members work to provide a home that is consistent in its expectations and in matters of discipline. The hearing-impaired child must be recognized and treated as a child first, and as a child with a hearing loss second.

*Sheryl L. Roesser*

# 9

# The Process of Language
# Stimulation and Development
# for Hearing-Impaired Children

Communication skills are necessary to interact effectively and appropriately with the world around us (Wood, 1976). Language has been referred to as a "tool" for communication. Actually, language can be defined in many ways, depending on how one perceives the meaning of the word. We do know that language is extremely important as it is the foundation upon which other skills, such as speech, reading, and writing, are built. We also know that, in reality, language is not a separate entity that can be learned without consideration of other aspects of the individual. Our personality, interests, maturational level, and amount of exposure to the world about us all lend to the development of language and are reflected by the manner in which we use it.

## THE IMPORTANCE OF EARLY INTERVENTION

Educators and other professionals are, or have become in recent years, increasingly aware of the necessity for early intervention whenever a child exhibits some type of exceptional characteristic that may interfere with the learning process. This awareness has been evidenced by an increase in the number of infant and preschool programs currently being provided for the exceptional child. Parent groups, professional groups, and recent legislative acts have all led to enhancing the importance of early intervention to educators, health care professionals, and the general public.

Early intervention for the hearing-impaired child is extremely important, particularly in the area of language development. From a biological point of view, all human beings have the innate ability to acquire language as long as severe limitations are not placed on its development (Lenneberg, 1969). It is also true that the first few years of life are crucial to language learning, and that without stimulation the innate ability to acquire such skills may be lost. The most obvious reason for the language delay in hearing-impaired children is the lack of auditory stimulation. This deprivation of the auditory channel inhibits the development of perceptual strategies necessary for language development (Bess, 1981). Early identification and intervention are the primary strategies, therefore, in assisting the hearing-impaired child in acquiring effective and appropriate communication skills.

In this chapter the importance of early identification and intervention is outlined to give the reader a basis from which to approach such a program, and to provide some general guidelines for improving the language skills of hearing-impaired children. The discussion that follows considers those factors in relationship to the congenitally severe (65–90dB) or profound (90dB and above) hearing-impaired child. Much of the information, with appropriate modification, may be applicable to the mild to moderate (15–65dB) hearing-impaired child. It is not the intention to provide an in-depth discussion of all aspects of the language learning process, but to present some information and guidelines for working with the young hearing-impaired child. The reader is encouraged to partake of additional study to enhance his or her knowledge of the terms and procedures mentioned. A suggested bibliography has been provided at the conclusion of the chapter for this purpose.

## LANGUAGE OF THE DEAF

There have been numerous investigations, utilizing a variety of methodologies, into the language abilities of the hearing impaired. These investigations have attempted to define specifically the language of the deaf to determine how their abilities deviate developmentally from those of hearing children, and the reasons such deviations exist. These investigations have also been conducted in an effort to assist educators in enhancing the hearing-impaired child's future language abilities.

What are the results of those investigations and what do we really know about the language of the deaf?

Ivimey (1982) reviews the investigations of several people, including those of Blanton (1967, 1971), Brannon (1968), Cohen (1965), Heider and Heider (1940), Moores (1970), Myklebust (1964), Simmons (1962), and Wells (1942). In his article Ivimey points out the various shortcomings that exist in previous investigations of deaf language, but he finishes the discussion with some general information that he believes reliable. He concludes that deaf children produce less language than do much younger hearing children regardless of the methods employed to measure the deaf child's abilities. Ivimey believes that deaf children show a preference for short, simple sentences rather than long, complex, or compound sentences. There is an overuse of nouns and verbs by the deaf and an underuse, or misuse, of auxiliaries, prepositions, determiners, and adverbs. Negative and interrogative sentences were reported as frequently incorrect, structurally. Each sentence employed by the deaf tends to form an isolated conceptual unit, and successive sentences rarely carry a single thought or group of thoughts.

Ivimey also concludes that teachers of the deaf are probably already familiar with the conclusions reported in his review of investigations and that this information does not assist the professional in designing specific language programs for the deaf child. These known facts do begin to explain which areas are deviant, but not why. Nor do they suggest solutions to the problem.

## LANGUAGE AS A MEANS OF COMMUNICATION

The term *language* is frequently conceived as "what someone has said" or as "spoken words." Although words are a major avenue for interacting within our environment, language involves more than the mere use of words. *Receptive language* includes how we perceive and interpret the thoughts, ideas, emotions, and feelings of others and, in general, the world around us. *Expressive language*, on the other hand, refers to how we convey, or communicate, these same aspects of ourselves to others (Bloom & Lahey, 1978; Sitnick, 1978; Wood, 1976). These two entities, receptive and expressive, are also inter-related in the general development of language. In other words, the quantity and quality of input (reception) will have a direct effect on the output (expression).

### Verbal and Nonverbal Channels of Communication

The use of both receptive and expressive language involves verbal and nonverbal channels of communication. *Verbal communication* does include the use of words for labeling and/or describing objects, thoughts, and feelings. However, the grouping of these words into phrases and sentences (syntactical units) aids in understanding and interpreting the meaning of the message. The use of additional words and the order in which they are presented reduce the options of the intended meaning for which a single word may present to the listener. The second general category, *nonverbal communication*, involves the characteristics of the speaker's voice and the use of body language. The voice characteristics (often referred to as the suprasegmentals or prosodic features of speech) include the pitch, intensity, duration, and intonational or inflectional patterns used by the speaker. Body language includes eye contact, facial expressions, body movements, gestures, and the distance the speaker maintains between himself and the listener (Webster, 1977; Wood, 1976). We consciously or unconsciously interpret a speaker's meaning, therefore, by analyzing a combination of various verbal and nonverbal aspects of the message.

The following example is used to illustrate the inter-relatedness of the verbal and nonverbal aspects of communication. The very young child frequently employs single words, such as "doggie," to communicate his or her thoughts. However, the person receiving the message needs additional information for accurate decoding of the intended message. Is the child simply naming the animal or checking his vocabulary accuracy? Is the child trying to convey a specific message related to the dog or does he or she simply want us to look at the discovery? The use of a syntactical structure, such as "bad doggie" provides information that the child may or may not feel the dog has done something wrong. The child may still be asking a question rather than passing judgment. Now the suprasegmentals of speech aid in clarifying the words as a statement rather than a question. For example, the child's pitch may be lowered in a scolding manner, a downward inflection on the word "doggie" distinguishes it as a declarative statement, and the loudness or intensity of the child's voice may indicate not only anger, but the degree of this emotion. The child's body language, including an angry face, clenched fists, and the forward movement with a mighty blow to the dog, also illustrates the child's anger and the intention for the animal to stop whatever he is doing.

### Congruent and Incongruent Messages

So far in our discussion of the verbal and nonverbal aspects of communication, we have assumed these were congruent messages. Congruency means that the various verbal and nonverbal aspects are in agreement with the intended message. Incongruent messages occur when there is a conflict between one or more of the various communication channels. Wood (1976) discusses the fact that sarcastic remarks and joking present problems to a 12-year-old hearing child, and even to some high school students, due to the complexity of sorting such a message. Just as the hearing juvenile may have difficulty understanding the incongruent message of an adult's sarcastic remark due to inexperience in decoding such messages, it is in this same manner that the hearing-impaired child has problems in interpreting simple congruent statements. Due to lack of exposure to the world about them, to the language employed by their hearing peers, and because of the auditory deprivation, the deaf frequently never acquire the ability to decode messages that carry new or extended meanings, or that differ from the literal.

Through this brief discussion of language, the reader will realize there are various channels of communication that depend heavily on both the auditory and visual senses. We not only hear the words, their ordering, and the voice of the speaker, but we can also observe the speaker's reaction. In addition to understanding the content and form of our language, the development of perceptual and cognitive skills related to our interactions with others and the world about us are necessary to develop appropriate and effective communication skills. Due to the auditory deficiency and to the fact that many important cognitive and perceptual skills are learned during the first few years of life, early identification and intervention for the young hearing-impaired child is extremely important for language development so that he or she will not be deprived of these necessary skills.

## EARLY IDENTIFICATION AND AMPLIFICATION

Techniques have been developed to identify the severely and profoundly hearing-impaired child during the neonatal stage of life. However, a nationwide commitment to use such procedures has not been established. Hearing-impaired children often remain undetected, therefore, until the age of 2 or 3 years (Bess, 1981). Hearing children of the same age are already exhibiting receptive and expressive language skills. Not only do they possess a well established vocabulary of environmental and functional words, but they are also demonstrating a knowledge of basic syntactical structures (Bloom & Lahey, 1978). At the time of diagnosis, therefore, the hearing-impaired child has already been deprived valuable information during critical learning years, and he or she will probably never be able to "catch-up" with hearing peers.

## Auditory Training

Once the child has been diagnosed and fitted with appropriate amplification, an auditory training program must be initiated. Some people are under the misconception that if a deaf child responds to an environmental sound or a speaker's voice through the use of a hearing aid, he or she is perceiving this information in the same manner as a hearing person. For the following reasons the purchase of a hearing aid usually does not alleviate the problem of hearing speech. Deaf children usually possess enough amplified residual hearing to detect loud, low-pitched environmental sounds and the presence of a speaker's voice at close range. However, due to the nature of the sensori-neural hearing loss, they are less able to detect higher frequency sounds. Many of the phonetic elements of speech, such as the /s, sh, th and f/ sounds, are produced within these higher frequencies, and unfortunately with less intensity than other low frequency speech sounds such as vowels. In other words, the child may hear the presence of a speaker's voice, but not be able to understand or discriminate individual speech sounds.

This does not mean that the auditory channel is an ineffective means for language development in the hearing-impaired child. With appropriate training the deaf child can learn to use the suprasegmentals of speech (the nonword aspects of speech) in comprehending spoken language. In other words, the child can learn to utilize prosodic information including pitch, rate, duration, intensity, and rhythmic patterns to aid in his or her ability to comprehend spoken language. The child can utilize this information to recognize familiar phrases before he or she understands each word in the message (Sitnick, 1978). Due to the hearing loss, the child will not be able to perceive speech as a hearing person. This, in turn, has a direct effect on his or her ability to acquire proficient speech skills. However, if the child is able to employ appropriate suprasegmentals within his or her own oral communication, the child's general intelligibility to the listener will be greatly enhanced.

The importance of the suprasegmentals of speech in the comprehension and expression of spoken language means that everyone in the child's environment should talk to him or her just as they would any other child. When talking with the hearing-impaired child, appropriate volume should be used. Shouting causes further distortion of speech. Interesting and varied intonational patterns should be used, and the child should be spoken to at a moderate rate, that is, not too slow nor too fast (Sitnick, 1978). Voice should be used to get the child's attention rather than constantly touching him or her. In this way, the child learns to respond to the human voice by looking and hopefully attending to conversations regardless of whether they are directed specifically toward him or her.

## EARLY INTERVENTION

Language learning must be interesting, motivating, and rewarding to the child. It is not something that can be totally and effectively taught to the very young hearing-impaired child through structured activities in the confines of a classroom or clinical setting. Very young children learn language on an ongoing basis throughout each day. Therefore, intervention strategies should be centered around the events of the child's day that interest him or her at the moment. The child also needs opportunities for self-initiated discovery and practice for language to become a meaningful, motivating, and rewarding means of communication. The importance of a wide variety of opportunities for interacting with others and with the environment should not be underestimated. It should be stressed for all concerned that the most natural and realistic environment for early language learning is in the home, community, and daily environment in which the child functions.

The amount of interaction, input, and opportunities the child has to express him or herself will also have a definite effect on the development of receptive and expressive language abilities. We cannot expect the child to learn language incidentally by hearing or "overhearing" the conversations of other people as do hearing children. Regardless of the communication approach adopted (oral, manual, or total communication), therefore, the child will need constant and consistent language stimulation throughout the entire day. The importance of maximizing language stimulation and experiences in the most natural and realistic environment lends itself to the fact that the child's main caretaker should be a primary intervention agent. This could naturally be the child's parent. Professionals and parents must work together as equal team members in order to enhance the language skills of the young hearing-impaired child.

As professionals, we can assist parents in developing intervention skills they already possess, but for which they may not presently be aware they have. This does not mean the professional should lay the responsibility solely on the parent(s). Nor does it mean that we merely describe the effects of a hearing loss, the general stage of language development, prescribe a course of action for the parents to take, and then expect them to follow through. Information sharing is an important part of the intervention program, both from the professional's input of technical information and from the parents' input on personal aspects of the child. In addition to information, however, parents will need demonstration of what is expected of them. It is much easier to follow someone's instructions if you have had adequate opportunity to observe them carrying out the task. Parents also need encouragement or reinforcement in that what they are doing is right. Whenever anyone attempts a new task, they are hesitant and unsure of their methods until they have acquired some experience and have been able to observe the fruits of their labor. Since language learning for the hearing-impaired child is going to be a life-long process, parents will need encouragement to take each day one step at a time, and reinforcement to continue on a daily basis in lieu of frustrated surrender (Kroth, 1972, 1975; Webster, 1977).

The above discussion was not presented to imply that all language intervention must take place in the home. There can be a harmonious combination of home and school or clinic learning. Regardless of the type of intervention program initiated, however, there must be coordinated consistency between activities presented in all learning settings. This also does not imply that parents must devote the rest of their lives to the language development of their children without any regard to their own needs as individuals. Jobs, other family members, friends, everyday chores, and personal pleasures cannot be ignored. It is more likely that happy, well-rounded, parents will promote a happy child. Parents should also remember that they need not, and should not, be the only home intervention agents. Everyone in the child's daily environment, such as siblings, grandparents, and friends, should take an active role in the language stimulation of the child.

### Home Language Development Activities

As previously mentioned, language is not something that can be taught effectively to the very young hearing-impaired child through structured activities, such as sitting at a table and identifying pictured objects for the purpose of vocabulary building. The child needs to be able to move around, touch, feel, manipulate, or be exposed to, the real object. To sit at a table and be presented with pictures of zoo or farm animals is not as meaningful, motivating, or interesting to the child as it is to actually observe these animals in their own natural habitat. "What is an elephant?" No matter how good the picture of an elephant might be, it cannot describe or depict the magnitude of the elephant's size, the way it moves, or the actual appearance of its wrinkly skin that may be experienced at the zoo. How it uses its trunk to lift food to its mouth or blow water over its back cannot be effectively described with pictures. This type of real observation lends "meaning" to the word elephant. Later, after such an experience, the child may be extremely interested in discussing a picture or storybook of an elephant, because now he or she has something to "talk about."

After such real-life experiences, the use of toys, pictures, and books may be appropriate in short, more structured activities. However, when utilizing pictorial representations, there are a few things the intervention agent should keep in mind. Pictures and books need to be simple, colorful, and true to life. In other words, pictures should not be cluttered or "busy" with additional objects other than the one being focused on during the lesson. Colorful pictures are also much more stimulating and interesting to a child than are black line drawings. Pictures should be true to life rather than caricature in nature and should resemble the real object in the child's environment as much as possible. Books should also depict factual life-like situations about real people, places, and activities rather than solely imaginery (fairy tale) situations.

## The Child's Day

The young hearing-impaired child's day is full of natural language learning situations. Due to the auditory deprivation, however, these situations require some restructuring and planning to maximize the child's receptive and expressive skills. Activities, such as dressing or bathing, are excellent opportunities for the child to learn clothing, body parts, or prepositions. It is much more interesting and meaningful to discuss *shoes, socks* or *pants* when actually performing the act of putting these objects *on* or taking them *off* your *legs* or *feet*. When bathing, the parent who is assisting in this task might discuss how it feels to have water trickle down the child's *back* or that they need to *wash* those *dirty hands*. This is not to say that the child should be bombarded with all these vocabulary words at once. Initially, the intervention agent should select one or two target words for each activity, adding additional vocabulary after the child has demonstrated some understanding of previously targeted words. Target words should not be taught in isolation. The child not only needs to be able to label objects, actions, and feelings, but also needs to be exposed to the use of syntactical structures and how the meaning of the message depends on the relationship of the words involved.

The child can also receive a wealth of language opportunities by assisting parents or siblings in the completion of household tasks. The unloading of a dishwasher or the setting of the table for a meal offers exposure to tableware vocabulary, such as *cup, glass, spoon,* or *fork,* and again the use of *prepositions,* such as *on* and *off,* or *over* and *under.* Helping dad rake the leaves stimulates conversation about *trees, grass, seasons of the year,* and the *weather.* To expand the child's knowledge beyond the immediate home environment, a trip may be planned for a walk or a ride in the car to the grocery store. Other trips might include going to a farm, a zoo, an airport, or the post office. A ride on the bus to the country, city, or to a friend's house may also be included. The possibilities of expanding the child's knowledge of his or her immediate and extended environment are endless. The reader who wishes to know more about how to implement these natural and planned experiences into the daily routine of the child is encouraged to refer to the *John Tracy Clinic Correspondence Course for Parents of Preschool Deaf Children* (Theilman, 1972) for additional information.

It will require additional time and effort to restructure daily activities to ensure language stimulation. However, it is time well spent. The reader should not be under the misconception that every daily event must be restructured. There are only so many hours within a day. And in addition to being time consuming, these restructured activities often require a great deal of patience on the part of both the intervention agent and the child.

### Limiting The Number of Activities

Language learning should be fun. Therefore, it is often better to reduce the number of learning activities within the span of a day rather than frustrating the participants. On the other hand, language opportunities need to be interesting, motivating, and without limitations. Educators and parents must scrutinize their methods to ensure these important elements of language learning. The child not only needs to be exposed to constant language learning situations, but also to ample opportunities to develop a self-motivating desire to express him or herself. This desire is obtained through self-realization that one can most efficiently and effectively manipulate his or her environment through formal language usage.

The following are suggestions for enhancing the language abilities of hearing-impaired children.

BE AN ACTIVE LISTENER.    Sometimes children's questions or efforts to communicate can be viewed as annoyances by adults. Children must want to communicate, however, and they must have ample opportunities to practice their skills. So give the child your undivided attention whenever possible. Let him or her know that you are interested. Make every effort to understand the child and let him or her know when you do. On the occasions you don't understand, be honest and make every effort to assist the child in clarifying the message. At times you may need to help the child express his or her thoughts or feelings, but talking for the child should be avoided.

BE A GOOD LANGUAGE MODEL.    Avoid the use of single words and "baby talk." Whenever the child says a word, either orally and/or manually, repeat it, and then expand the word into a sentence. In the early stages of language development use short, simple, but complete sentences. Later in language development expand the words into a sentence by using new and varied sentence forms. Extend the word by providing new vocabulary, additional information, and examples of multiple meanings in a single word.

BE A GOOD FACILITATOR OF LANGUAGE. Talk to the child as much as possible whenever he or she is looking. Talk about whatever interests the child at the moment. However, don't make the child look at you. Everything has a name—use it. If the child does not understand what you want him or her to do, show him. Sign and/or speak all conversations when the child is present.

BE A GOOD VISUAL MODEL. Be at the child's eye level whenever possible. Make sure the light is not in the child's eyes, or that an object is obstructing his or her view. Speak and/or sign distinctly, but do not exaggerate in any way. Lip reading is based on normal speech. Use natural gestures and body language.

BE A GOOD AUDITORY MODEL. Speak at a moderate rate and with appropriate volume. Use varied and interesting intonational patterns. Reward the child for using his or her voice. Encourage the child to use voice to get your attention.

BE PATIENT. Remember that no two children are alike and that each child develops at his or her own rate. Language development norms for hearing children may be used as guidelines for working with the hearing-impaired child, but remember that age at which amplification and intervention were initiated must be considered rather than chronological age. Also, hearing-impaired children do not necessarily develop their language skills in the same order as other children, and frequently they progress more slowly from one stage to the next.

## SUMMARY

Due to the auditory deprivation imposed by the severity of a deaf child's hearing loss, the ability to develop effective and appropriate communication skills is an extremely difficult and time-consuming process. We can assist these children in obtaining this goal through earlier identification, amplification, and intervention in the most natural environment.

By being exposed to meaningful language experiences in real-life situations, the child is able to build important cognitive and perceptual skills necessary for language development. In addition, educators and parents must continue working together in search of additional language

THE HEARING-IMPAIRED CHILD IN SCHOOL

intervention strategies and efficient methodologies that enhance the deaf child's abilities.

## REFERENCES

Bess, F. H., & McConnell, F. E. Audiology, education, and the hearing impaired child. St. Louis: C. V. Mosby Company, 1981.

Blanton, R. L., Nunally, J. C., & Odom, P. Psycholinguistic processes in the deaf. Cyclostyled, Vanderbilt University, 1967.

Blanton, R. L., Odom, P. B., & McIntyre, C. W. Symbolic and linguistic processes in the deaf. Cyclostyled, Vanderbilt University, 1971.

Bloom, L., & Lahey, M. Language development and language disorders. New York: John Wiley & Sons, 1978.

Brannon, J. B. Linguistic word classes in the spoken language of normal, hard of hearing and deaf children. Journal of Speech and Hearing Research, 1968, 2(2), 279–287.

Cohen, S. R. Redundancy in the written language of the deaf. In Rosenstein, J. & McGinitie, W. H., Research studies on the psycholinguistic behavior of deaf children. Washington, D.C.: Council for Exceptional Children, 1965.

Heider, F. K., & Heider, G. M. A comparison of the sentence structure of deaf and hearing children. Psychological Monographs, 1940, (52), 42–103.

Horton, K. B. Home demonstration teaching for parents of very young deaf children. Volta Review, 1968, 70, 97–104.

Ivimey, G. P. Assessing the language skills of hearing-impaired children—a critical review. Journal of the British Association for Teachers of the Deaf, 1982, 6(5), 133–144.

Kroth, R. L. Communicating with parents of exceptional children. Denver: Love, 1975.

Kroth, R. L. Facilitating educational progress by improving parent conferences. Focus On Exceptional Children, 1972, 4(7), 1–10.

Lenneberg, E. On explaining language. Science, 1969, 164, 635–643.

Lloyd, L. L. Communication assessment and intervention strategies. Baltimore: University Park Press, 1976.

Moores, D. F. An investigation of the psycholinguistic functioning of deaf adolescents. Exceptional Children, 1970, 36(9), 645–652.

Myklebust, H. R. The psychology of deafness. New York: Grune & Stratton, 1964.

Simmons, A. A. A comparison of the type-token ratio of spoken and written language of deaf and hearing children. Volta Review, 1962, 64(7), 417–421.

Sitnick, V., Rushmer, N., & Arpan, R. Parent–infant communication: a program of clinical and home training for parents and hearing impaired infants. Oregon:Dormac, 1978.

Theilman, V. B., Director & Staff. John Tracy clinic correspondence course for parents of preschool deaf children. Los Angeles: John Tracy Clinic, 1972.

Webster, E. J. Counseling with parents of handicapped children. New York: Grune & Stratton, 1977.

Wells, C. O. The development of abstract language concepts in normal and deaf children. Chicago: University of Chicago Libraries, 1942.

Wood, B. S. Children and communication: verbal and nonverbal language. Englewood Cliffs, New Jersey: Prentice-Hall, 1976.

## BIBLIOGRAPHY

Bloom, F. Our Deaf Children. Washington, D.C.: A. G. Bell Association for the Deaf, 1963.

Calvert, D. R., & Silverman, S. R. Speech and Deafness. Washington, D.C.: A. G. Bell Association for the Deaf, 1975.

Furth, H. G. *Deafness and Learning: A Psychological Approach.* Belmont, Calif.: Wadsworth Publishing Company, Inc., 1973.

Northcott, W. *Curriculum Guide, Hearing-Impaired Children—Birth to Three Years—and Their Parents.* Washington, D.C.: A. G. Bell Association for the Deaf, 1972.

Northcott, W. Language development through parent counseling and guidance. *Volta Review,* 1966, 68, pp. 356–360.

Northern, J. L., & Downs, M. P. *Hearing in Children.* Baltimore: Williams and Wilkins, 1974.

Pollack, D. *Educational Audiology for the Limited Hearing Infant.* Springfield, Illinois: Charles C. Thomas, 1970.

Rollins, J. C. I heard that! Auditory training at home, *Volta Review* reprint no. 983. Washington, D.C.: A. G. Bell Association for the Deaf, 1972.

Schiefelbusch, L., & Lloyd, L. L. *Language Perspectives, Retardation, and Intervention.* Baltimore: University Park Press, 1974.

Vygotsky, L. S. *Thought and Language.* Cambridge, Mass.: M.I.T. Press, 1962.

*Cheryl DeConde*

# 10

# Children with Central Auditory Processing Disorders

The ability to attend to spoken conversation, to comprehend, remember, and relate what is heard so that appropriate responses can be made involves a series of intricate processes that occur automatically in most individuals. Rarely does one consider the complex succession of events that is involved in the integration of information in our brain during conversation. For effective communication to occur, the brain, through the central nervous system network, must receive, transmit, decode, sort, and organize all auditory information before comprehension is achieved. This integration must take place in a rapid and precise manner even when background noise and other alterations of the auditory signal (manner of speaking and environment) create interference. The anatomical network and redundancies of the auditory neural pathways work as an intricate mechanism to perform these functions.

Central auditory processing (CAP) is the current label ascribed to this neurological phenomenon. Central auditory processing dysfunction, auditory perceptual disorder, and minimal brain dysfunction are names used to describe the problem that some individuals experience. Efficient and accurate auditory processing skills are particularly crucial to children, because deficits most often result in reading problems (Bakker & deWit, 1977; Kaluger & Kolson, 1969; Knox & Roesser, 1980; Rampp,

THE HEARING-IMPAIRED CHILD IN SCHOOL
ISBN 0-8089-1663-7

1980; Tarnopol & Tarnopol, 1977), and reading skill is probably the best predictor of success in school (Kurland & Colodny, 1969; Rampp, 1980; Yule & Rutter, 1976). Significant auditory processing problems can also cause delays in speech and language development (Butler, 1981; Protti, Young, & Byrne, 1980). The hierarchy of events that lead to normal acquisition of skills necessary for reading, and ultimately to a successful student, are dependent on fast, efficient processing of auditory information.

## RELATIONSHIP OF CENTRAL AUDITORY PROCESSING DISORDERS TO LEARNING DISABILITIES

The term *learning disability* was first used by S. A. Kirk in 1962 to describe the cause of a discrepancy between a child's achievement level and his capacity to learn. In 1969, the following definition was adopted by Congress as the basis of the 1969 Learning Disabilities Act and subsequently was included in Public Law 94–142 (1975):

> The term "children with specific learning disabilities" means those children who have a disorder in one or more of the basic psychological processes involved in understanding or in using language, spoken or written, which disorder may manifest itself in imperfect ability to listen, think, speak, read, write, spell, or do mathematical calculations. Such disorders include such conditions as perceptual handicaps, brain injury, minimal brain dysfunction, dyslexia, and developmental aphasia. Such term does not include children who have learning problems which are primarily the result of visual, hearing, or motor handicaps, of mental retardation, of emotional disturbance, or environmental, cultural or economic disadvantage (Federal Register, 1977).

Many attempts at revising this definition have been made since the early 1970s, but no consensus was ever reached. The above definition still stands as government policy.

More recently, in an attempt to redefine, clarify, and redirect the focus of learning disabilities, representatives of the American Speech, Language, and Hearing Association, the Association for Children with Learning Disabilities, the Council for Learning Disabilities of the Council for Exceptional Children, the Division for Children with Communication Disorders of the Council for Exceptional Children, the International Reading Association, and the Orton Dyslexia Society formed the National Joint Committee on Learning Disabilities. After extensive debate, they proposed the following definition:

Learning Disabilities is a generic term that refers to a heterogeneous group of disorders manifested by significant difficulties in the acquisition and use of listening, speaking, reading, writing, reasoning, or mathematical abilities. These disorders are intrinsic to the individual and presumed to be due to central nervous system dysfunction. Even though a learning disability may occur concomitantly with other handicapping conditions (e.g., sensory impairment, mental retardation, social and emotional disturbances) or environmental influences (e.g., cultural differences, insufficient/inappropriate instruction, psychogenic factors), it is not the direct result of those conditions or influences. (Hammill, Larsen, Leigh, & McNutt, 1981, p. 336).

The focus of this definition was to emphasize the severity and heterogenity of learning disabilities. The committee recommended that discussion and application to determine its effect on diagnosis and services to learning-disabled students would be necessary before it could be considered for adoption as the new definition. It was admitted that central auditory processing dysfunction is one of the neurologic disorders that leads to or contributes to the learning problem and is present in many learning-disabled children.

## Prevalence Statistics

Prevalence statistics refer to the number of children who actually exist with a certain handicap. Gearheart and Weishan (1976) reported a prevalence rate of learning disabled children of 2.0 to 4.0 percent of the population ages 5 to 18 based on a compilation of state and federal reports. In a more recent survey (Tucker, Stevens, & Ysseldyke, 1983), the largest number of respondents (21.0 percent) believed that 3 percent of school-age children were learning disabled, still consistent with the 1976 statistics. Learning disabilities are also more common in boys than girls by a ratio of about 4:1. A common concern has centered around the rise in numbers of learning-disabled children over the past few years. Two conditions may explain this fact: first, the presence of more proficient diagnostic skills; and second, due to medical advances, more infants are surviving high risk birth conditions, but with residual neurologic impairment as a result of those conditions.

Determination of the percent of learning-disabled children who have central auditory processing disorders is difficult to discern primarily due to the lack of standardized definitions and identification procedures. Additionally, it has only been within the last 5 years that enough widespread interest has been generated in this area to begin to compile meaningful statistics. Obviously as expertise develops in the identification of central auditory processing problems, more children, particularly those with milder difficulties, will be identified. Further confusion occurs from the variability that is evidenced in the auditory performance of young children (to about age 8) due to developmental and other factors.

## HEARING ACUITY VERSUS CENTRAL AUDITORY PROCESSING

It is imperative to distinguish between the peripheral (acuity) and central (perceptual) parameters in the diagnosis of auditory disorders. Hearing acuity describes a person's sensitivity to sound; that is, one's ability to receive and detect the presence of even very faint tones at various pitches. The integration of the information that is heard is the second and equally important step in the total process of hearing. Both aspects must be considered when the evaluation of hearing ability occurs. A child may have deficits in one or both areas. Auditory processing deficiencies are difficult to separate diagnostically from the problems of reduced hearing acuity when they occur simultaneously. It is, however, the responsibility of the audiologist to determine the child's capabilities in each area whenever possible. Unfortunately many audiologists and audiology clinics still do not recognize the importance of the central auditory processing evaluation. As a result, the presence of a central auditory processing problem may not be considered when a hearing test rules out peripheral hearing loss.

### Relationship to Classroom Performance

Children with central auditory processing disorders often exhibit the classroom symptoms of the child with mild to moderate and perhaps fluctuating hearing loss. Their behavior is often quite inconsistent, particularly as it revolves around auditory skills such as discrimination, remembering, and comprehending information. For a teacher this behavior can be exasperating, especially when it is unclear whether the child is purposefully inattentive or possesses a physiological basis for such actions. Academically the child may have difficulties that predominate in reading or math, or both. The child may demonstrate neither symptom. However, phonetic development and other reading readiness skills seem to be the primary academic area of concern for young school-age children. Socially the child may exhibit inappropriate behavior as a result of the mental confusion created by the central auditory processing problem. These children become quite frustrated or anxious and, therefore, may be aggressive with other children or withdrawn. Early diagnosis is crucial so that persons in the child's environment are aware of the child's needs and make necessary adaptations to accommodate them as well as to implement appropriate intervention programs.

## Specific Auditory Abilities

It is not uncommon to see auditory processing separated into individual components. Keith (1981) compiled these important auditory abilities:

DISCRIMINATION.    To differentiate among sounds of different frequency, duration, or intensity.

LOCALIZATION.    To localize the source of sound.

AUDITORY ATTENTION.    To pay attention to auditory signals, especially speech, for an extended time.

AUDITORY FIGURE-GROUND.    To identify a primary speaker from a background noise.

AUDITORY DISCRIMINATION.    To discriminate among words and sounds that are acoustically similar.

AUDITORY CLOSURE.    To understand the whole message when part is missing.

AUDITORY BLENDING.    To synthesize isolated phonemes embedded in words.

AUDITORY ANALYSIS.    To identify phonemes or morphemes embedded in words.

AUDITORY ASSOCIATION.    To identify a sound with its source.

AUDITORY MEMORY, SEQUENTIAL MEMORY.    To store and recall auditory stimuli of different length or number in exact order (p. 160).

Although these abilities represent different aspects of the processing continuum and can be defined discreetly, one must question if they can be dealt with in isolation or are mutually exclusive for either diagnostic or remediation purposes. Auditory information processing involves all of these skills simultaneously. Caution must be used when these functions are identified independently.

## BASES OF CENTRAL AUDITORY PROCESSING PROBLEMS

### Neurological Functioning

The complex integrative task of assimilating auditory information is accomplished via a network consisting of the auditory neural pathways within the brainstem and cortex. All identifiable brain structures are present at birth, but single cell development continues, increasing the complexity of each cell's dendritic structures and expanding their connections with other neurons. This dendritic elaboration occurs with and allows for increased information processing capabilities. Complete maturation of the central nervous system may continue until puberty.

For over three decades it has been documented that crossed (contralateral) auditory neural pathways are dominant over uncrossed (ipsilateral) ones; about 70 percent of the fibers cross to the opposite side of the brain while 30 percent remain on the same side (Rosenzweiz, 1951; Tunturi, 1946). Therefore, auditory information received through the right ear is directed to the left hemisphere of the cortex, and input to the left ear is directed to the right hemisphere. For most people the left temporal lobe is dominant for processing linguistic information (also mathematical computations and analysis, and logical and analytic thinking), while the right temporal lobe predominates for the processing of nonlinguistic information (including musical development, spatial relations, imagination, dance and sculpture, and visual perception). This processing paradigm is supported by the fact that Wernicke's area (the primary receiving station for gross interpretation of sound) in the temporal lobe has been shown to be anatomically larger on the left side in 65 percent of brains and larger on the right side in only 7 percent (Geschwind & Levitzky, 1968). Therefore, the fact that most people use their right-hand and right-ear is a critical component of the cross-over of sensory information to the opposite side. This hemispheric specialization, with specific emphasis on processing asymmetries in the auditory system, has led to several theories relating failure of the left hemisphere to predominate for language functions to dyslexia (Bakker, 1969; Orton, 1925; Zangwill, 1960).

Much of the analysis and sorting of input that occurs within the brainstem facilitates directing the appropriate information to the pertinent hemisphere for auditory processing to proceed in its most efficient manner. Speaks (1975) has adapted a model shown in Figure 10-1 that depicts this information processing model. The solid lines represent the contralateral pathways while the dashed lines are the ipsilateral ones. The ear signals travel to the opposite temporal lobes; in the right temporal lobe a preliminary auditory analysis occurs where information

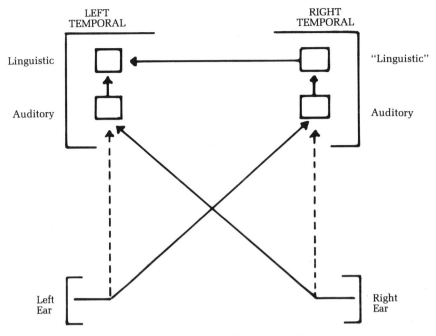

**Figure 10-1.** Contralateral and ipsilateral pathways for auditory processing. (Reproduced from Speaks, C. Dichotic listening: a clinical or research tool? In M. Sullivan (Ed.), *Processing of a symposium on central auditory processing disorders.* Omaha, Nebraska: University of Nebraska Medical Center, 1975, p. 4.) With permission.

from the left ear that is linguistic is routed to the left temporal lobe, while nonlinguistic information is retained for analysis.

Information to the right ear travels to the left temporal lobe where both auditory and linguistic processing occur, resulting in a more direct and precise pathway for the linguistic signals. Further interconnections of fibers occur throughout the cortex that provides communication between the two hemispheres. Due to the many two-way connections, a large part of the cortex is involved in the processing of auditory information. The various cortical activities lead to the final perception and cognition of auditory information, which is necessary for the normal development of language and subsequent language-based processes.

## Organic and Nonorganic Factors

Many of the same factors that can cause hearing impairment in children can also result in central nervous system damage. In fact, the neurologic system at the level of the brain is even more susceptible to insult due to the longer and more extensive development period. Specific etiological correlates are nearly impossible to substantiate except in cases of diagnosed organic brain disorders. In central auditory processing disorders, lesions usually cannot be documented through histologic, radiologic, or even neurologic examinations. With many learning-disabled children, multiple factors probably interact to cause the observed learning deficiencies.

The prenatal period is extremely crucial for normal central nervous system development. Research studies have shown that prenatal trauma or complications are much more prevalent in children with neuropsychiatric disorders (Pasamanick & Knoblock, 1960) and in children who have learning difficulties (Colligan, 1974). Fetal malnutrition has been found to cause a permanent reduction in the number of cells in the central nervous system, thereby limiting brain function necessary for learning (Birch, 1971). Other conditions such as insufficient oxygen or breathing difficulties, low birth weight, prematurity, toxemia, drugs, and smoking are all potential sources for central nervous system impairment at birth. Although not documented, familial history of learning problems may also represent a predisposition factor for central auditory processing disorders.

Organically based brain dysfunction may occur postnatally as a result of trauma or disease or from any of the prenatal problems indicated above. Such organic disturbances as meningitis, seizure disorders, mental retardation, and cerebral palsy are common causes of brain damage. Organic lesions must produce measurable central nervous system symptoms or be in accompaniment with a history of one of the above problems as well as exhibiting evidence of specific behavioral deficits (disordered behavior, short attention span, emotional ability, social incompetence, defective work habits, impulsiveness, and meddlesomeness (Northern & Downs, 1978).

Nonorganic auditory processing disorders may be a result of environmental deprivation or minimal auditory deprivation when these conditions occur during the first 2 years of life. Northern & Downs (1978) cite lack of adequate stimulation, sensory overloading, and malnutrition as environmental factors, while minimal auditory deprivation is caused by the fluctuating hearing levels associated with middle ear effusion resulting in reduced neuronal development. These nonorganic disorders have been shown to result in irreversible impairment to the central auditory pathways.

It has only been within the last few years that the fluctuating hearing loss that accompanies chronic middle ear disease has been found to have a significant effect on auditory learning skills. The inconsistencies in input caused by the abnormal hearing levels may create delayed development in the child's ability to respond to, localize, attend to, and

**Table 10-1** *Relationship of Episodes of Otitis Media by Age and Sex in Children With vs Without Central Auditory Processing Disorders*

| Age | Number of Episodes | | | | | | |
|---|---|---|---|---|---|---|---|
| | CAP | | | Normal | | | |
| | Boys | Girls | Total | Boys | Girls | Total | |
| 0–1 years | 9 | 3 | 12 | 3 | 4 | 7 | |
| 1–2 | 12 | 6 | 18 | 5 | 4 | 9 | |
| 2–3 | 14 | 4 | 18 | 4 | 1 | 5 | |
| 3–4 | 13 | 7 | 20 | 1 | 0 | 1 | |
| 4–5 | 14 | 10 | 24 | 1 | 0 | 1 | |
| 5–6 | 16 | 12 | 28 | 0 | 0 | 0 | |
| 6–7 | 8 | 4 | 12 | 0 | 0 | 0 | |
| Total | 86 | 46 | 132 | 14 | 9 | 23 | |

comprehend auditory information. These may result in overall language and learning delays well after the child's middle ear problems have been resolved. Several research studies (Clark, 1980; Holm & Kunz, 1969; Katz, 1978; Lewis, 1976; Needleman, 1977; Webster & Webster, 1977) have produced alarming evidence of this problem; only recently have these been brought to the attention of physicians, parents, and educators.

An unpublished investigation (DeConde & McCarthy, 1980) conducted in the Greeley Public Schools examined the incidence of middle ear pathology in learning-disabled students who had diagnosed central auditory processing disorders. The physicians of each child in the matched control and experimental groups (10 boys, 10 girls each group) were contacted and asked to report from their records the number of episodes of middle ear pathology from birth to 7 years of age. A comparison of the two groups (see Table 10–1) indicated a total of 132 episodes for the central auditory processing group over the 7-year period, while only 23 episodes were reported for the control group. This was a statistically significant finding as it related to the number with CAP disorders. The number of episodes in boys outnumbered those in girls by approximately 2:1. An interesting finding of the study was the increased number of episodes at the 5 to 6-year range, which is contrary to most reports that show the incidence of otitis media greatest between 0 and 3 years. It can be hypothesized that this increase was due to the medical referrals that occurred as a result of the school hearing screening program prior to which many incidences may have gone undetected. Middle ear effusion (otitis media) is perhaps the most common childhood disease and the most controversial in treatment. As physicians debate medical treatment procedures, many children have become at risk for learning problems as a result of their early history of this disease, particularly when it has been allowed to linger over periods of several weeks or months.

## CHARACTERISTICS OF CENTRAL AUDITORY PROCESSING DISORDERS

The most prevalent behavior among the children with central auditory processing disorders is the inconsistencies that they demonstrate. Their processing ability, and consequently learning ability, is influenced by the environment, the structure through which information is presented, as well as their own attention, comprehension, and memory skills. Each child may appear to function normally at times while exhibiting problems on other occasions. The following characteristics are common in children who have central auditory processing problems:

1.  Seventy-five percent are male (Cohen, 1980).
2.  Hearing acuity is usually normal, although children with hearing impairments may also have central auditory processing problems. The child may exhibit considerable difficulty attending to the pure tone stimuli of the hearing evaluation and, therefore, show a significant discrepancy between pure tone averages and speech reception thresholds.
3.  They may be able to attend for only short periods of time or intermittently. They become fatigued or distracted when required to attend for longer periods of time.
4.  They may show difficulty following auditory directions.
5.  They may be easily distracted by sounds, voices, and movement. Since these children cannot block out irrelevant stimuli, they continually respond to incoming information.
6.  They may have difficulty remembering information presented verbally in both short-term and long-term memory.
7.  They often ask for information to be repeated.
8.  They may appear hyperactive. This may be due to their inability to store the meaning of sound in their brain so that they must constantly reinvestigate stimuli that are heard, resulting in complusive activity.
9.  They comprehend poorly what is heard or read.
10.  They may show delays in speech and language development.
11.  They may self-isolate themselves by retreating to a less confusing or distracting space.
12.  They may be easily frustrated, lack self-confidence, or be a behavior problem.
13.  They often perform below their expected grade level.
14.  They often have a significant history of middle ear pathology.

Some children may exhibit only one of the above symptoms while others may exhibit all of these behaviors. Obviously the more problems a child demonstrates, the more significant the processing disorder. It is also likely that the child who demonstrates obvious symptoms would be identified at an earlier age, while the child with more subtle difficulties may not be evident until his academic performance is questioned in third or fourth grade, or until his behavior problems are investigated in junior high school. These children may also have difficulties in fine and gross motor tasks and with visual perceptual functioning.

In summary, children with central auditory processing disorders have difficulty understanding verbal material that is presented under less than favorable listening conditions. On the other hand, in a quiet room and in a one to one speaker and listener situation, they compensate well and appear to function quite normally. Many children are not identified until they enter school where they must perform in much more complex learning situations than were present in their home environments.

## DIAGNOSIS OF CENTRAL AUDITORY PROCESSING PROBLEMS

### The Hearing Evaluation

Every central auditory processing assessment must begin with a hearing evaluation to rule out peripheral hearing loss. Subjective judgments can also be made at this time regarding the child's ability to attend to pure tone stimuli and general attention capabilities necessary for administering the central auditory processing battery. Additionally, precise hearing thresholds must be obtained to administer the central auditory processing test at standardized loudness levels. Compensation can be made for slight abnormalities in hearing levels, but when significant hearing loss or high frequency hearing loss exists, the central auditory processing battery should not be administered. When conductive hearing loss is present, testing should be postponed until normal thresholds are restored. Although a child appears behaviorally to exhibit a processing deficit in addition to an acuity problem, diagnostic validation is virtually impossible with the current measurement techniques. Diagnosis may not be that critical in terms of providing environmental modifications, however, since the practices are quite similar for both disorders.

### Health Developmental History

The health and developmental history is helpful in establishing the presence of any high risk factors that may contribute to central auditory processing disorders. This questionnaire must be filled out with the parent and includes specific questions regarding pregnancy and birth; medical and health data, including diseases of the ear, motor development, social development, educational history, and academic performance; and specific auditory behavior. The parent should be given an opportunity to express any other concerns, and at this time the purpose of the evaluation should be explained. Information from this history may be particularly useful in differentiating problem areas and in making recommendations for the home and classroom.

### Assessment

There are two distinct and different approaches to assessing auditory processing function. One is the more traditional approach that is used by speech and language pathologists, learning disabilities specialists, and psychologists. It involves assessing the specific auditory abilities (such as those indicated previously) presumed to be involved in language acquisition and the development of reading (Keith, 1981). Experts from these areas (Heasley, 1974; Kottler, 1972; Rampp, 1972; Reagan, 1973) have felt that the auuditory processing problems cause the language and learning problems and that remediation would then involve training through a hierarchy of processing skills. Another view expoused by Rees (1973) is that poor language competence causes the auditory processing problems and therefore, remediation is language based.

Some cautions must be discussed in regard to these assessment and remediation procedures. First, all of the tests used traditionally in this manner (including the Illinois Test of Psycholinguistic Abilities, the Goldman-Fristoe-Woodcock Auditory Discrimination and Selective Attention Tests, the Wepman Auditory Discrimination Test, the Composite Auditory Perceptual Test, the Lindamood Auditory Conceptualization Test, the Flowers-Costello Tests of Central Auditory Abilities, the Wechsler Intelligence Scale for Children) are language based. Therefore, performance is usually related to the level of language skill of the child and his or her educational background. Additionally, many of the tests utilize visual stimuli, usually pictures, which further detract from the auditory intent and pureness of the diagnostic task. A third problem is the lack of control in the presentation of these instruments. Only one, the Flowers-Costello Tests of Central Auditory Abilities, has a means for monitoring the presentation level so that some test-retest reliability can be measured. These variables are further confounded by the fact that auditory processes do not function in the pure form that the components are defined. It is difficult to discern then, exactly how and what these traditional assessment instruments are measuring.

The need for diagnostic procedures that assess the overall integrity of the central auditory system with emphasis on the focus of the particular problem within the auditory pathways is evident. This approach has been taken in the second assessment technique (Keith, 1981), which is typically performed by audiologists. In this battery of tests, the child's ability to perform auditorily under different conditions of signal distortion or competition is assessed (Keith, 1981). All tasks involve repetition of information that is heard, and they vary in length from consonant-vowel combinations to sentences. All tests are administered through a diagnostic audiometer in a soundproof room at precisely controlled intensities relative to the child's hearing thresholds. Because of the complexity and redundancy of the central auditory system, a variety of tests are administered to assess both brainstem and cortical functioning within the brain. Test results are then compared to standardized age norms for interpretation. Table 10–2 provides a brief description of the standard tests of the central auditory processing battery.

**Table 10-2** *Standard Tests of the Central Auditory Processing Battery*

*Willeford Battery*

| | |
|---|---|
| Ipsilateral-Contralateral Competing Sentence Test (I-C/CST) (Willeford & Billger, 1982) | Sumultaneously presented sentences of similar content presented in contralateral mode (−15dB message to competition ratio), ipsilateral mode (equal or −5dB message to competition ratio), and binaural mode (equal message to competition ratio) utilizing male vs female voice. Contralateral mode assesses cortical function, ipsilateral mode assesses brainstem function. Standardized norms 6 years–adult. |
| Binaural Competing Sentences (Willeford, 1968) | Simultaneously presented sentences of similar content; subject responds to the primary message which is 15dB softer than the competing message. Assesses cortical function where poor ear performance is contralateral to affected side. Performance between ears should be equal by 9 years. |
| Filtered Speech (Willeford, 1968) | Monotic discrimination of filtered consonant, nucleus, consonant words; filtering allows only frequencies below 500Hz to pass. Assesses cortical function where poor ear performance is contralateral to affected side. Performance between ears should be equal by 9 years. |
| Binaural Fusion (Ivey, 1969) | Spondee words presented such that a low frequency band segment (500–700Hz) is presented to one ear and simultaneously a high frequency band segment (1900–2100Hz) of the same word is presented to the opposite ear. Inability to resynthesize is indicative of upper brainstem dysfunction; performance between ears should be equal by 9 years. |
| Alternating Speech Perception (Willeford, 1968) | Sentences are presented in alternating bursts of 300 ms durations, first to one ear and then to the other. Typically a very easy task, but if performance is poor, it is indicative of lower brainstem dysfunction. |
| Staggered Spondaic Word Test (SSW) (Katz, 1973) | Spondee words are presented dichotically in a partially overlapping manner. |

|  | #1 | #2 | #3 |
|---|---|---|---|
| **Right Ear** | UP | STAIRS | |
| **Left Ear** | | DOWN | TOWN |
| | non-competing | competing | non-competing |
| | | | competing |

Assess cortical function; performance between ears should be equal by 10 years.

| Synthetic Sentence Identification (SSI) (Jerger, Speaks, & Trammel, 1968) | Linguistically constructed nonsense sentences interspersed periodically as the primary message and a continuous speech discourse (Davy Crockett Story) as the competing message. Presented at 0, −10, and −20dB message to competition ratios. When presented contralaterally assesses cortical function; ipsilateral presentation assesses brainstem function. Scoring is based on average of three message to competition ratios. Performance between ears should be equal by 10 years. |
| Compressed WIPI (Beasley, 1977) | The Word Intelligibility by Picture Identification (WIPI) Test is time compressed by 0%, 30%, and 60% and presented monaurally. Poor performance, usually at 60% time compression, may be indicative of cortical dysfunction on contralateral side. |
| Dichotic CV's (Berlin, 1973) | Paired CV syllables (pa, ta, ka, ba, da, ga) are presented simultaneously to each ear; they may be a directed response of right or left ear, or undirected. Poor performance in the directed response mode is representative of cortical dysfunction in the contralateral side. |
| Flowers-Costello Tests of Central Auditory Abilities (Flowers & Costello, 1970) Low Pass Filtered Speech | Child is presented sentence that is completed by pointing to correct picture. All speech sounds above 960Hz are filtered out, creating a low pass filtered speech stimulus. A low score indicates difficulty synthesizing auditory information. |
| Competing Messages | Child is presented sentence that is completed by pointing to correct picture. Sentences are interspersed while a story is told; both presented at equal loudness levels. A low score may indicate overall auditory perceptual difficulties, language development problems, and difficulties in background noise. Results are combined to obtain one score. Norms are provided for K–6th grades. |

### Interpretation

Although the development of the central auditory tests described above is primarily predicated on work with adult patients with organically based tumors or other neurological insults, they represent the state of the art at this time. Their use with children is supported by the growing concern of teachers, parents, psychologists, and other school and community persons with the dilemma these children present educationally, particularly when all other evidence may indicate normal potential. As a result, the use of these tests is increasing, and although there is still a great deal to learn about interpretation, the data from these evaluations can be analyzed and the instruments further developed. Due to the complexity of the auditory system, this assessment must entail a comprehensive battery approach where each test represents a slightly different processing task. Additionally, the results must be interpreted sensibly and in conjunction with other test data, such as the psychological, speech and language, and achievement status of the child. At this point in time these tests cannot identify specific language, learning, or reading deficits, nor can they provide remedial strategies for impairments in these areas. However, with continued investigation and research in auditory processing in children, the understanding and knowledge of causative factors may provide insight into remedial directions as well as improved assessment procedures.

The cultural and linguistic background of the child must be considered in interpretation. Because the central auditory processing tests are dependent on knowledge of language (English), bilingual children should be assessed in their primary language (Spanish versions of some central auditory processing tests are available) whenever possible. Bilingual children and language disordered children may require additional time or other modifications of the test situation. Interpretation must be cautious so that processing abilities are evaluated rather than the child's test-taking skills.

The test results often relate quite well to the classroom performance of the child. Certain central auditory processing tests appear to be more indicative of distractability or background noise problems, whereas others seem to relate to phonetic and auditory discrimination skills. This perception has not been established empirically by any of the authors of the individual tests and is based on observation by this author. The degree to which a child has difficulty on the central auditory processing battery also usually relates to the severity of the problems that are experienced. This relationship is difficult to predict, however, because a subtle problem diagnosed in one child may present significant processing difficulties in the classroom, while another child with more pronounced central auditory processing disorders may have acquired better compensation abilities and as a result function more adequately in the classroom.

Children with diagnosed central auditory processing disorders should be re-evaluated periodically (at least every two years) to monitor their auditory abilities. Due to the developmental nature of processing skills, test results may be used to measure the maturational level of the auditory pathways in addition to processing skills. Normal processing ability is attained eventually by some children, while others improve with age but never acquire adequate skills.

## MANAGEMENT OF STUDENTS WITH AUDITORY PROCESSING PROBLEMS

Good management techniques are crucial for the child with central auditory processing disorders. Because the research is inconclusive in the debate of whether or not specific remediation can be effective in restoring or developing central nervous system fibers, the usefulness of such training programs is certainly suspect. Adaptation of the child's environment, intensive language stimulation for young children, individualized instruction programs, and the teaching of compensatory skills and listening strategies for older children constitute the primary methods for treating central auditory processing disorders.

### At School

Following the central auditory processing evaluation, a conference should be arranged with the child's classroom teacher(s) to discuss test results and recommendations. It is also helpful to have a written handout or report of the recommendations to leave with the teacher. Often this conference is part of the special education staffing where results from all evaluations conducted are discussed by the team, child needs are determined, and appropriate services are established. The following recommendations have been successful with students who have central auditory processing disorders:

1. Seat the child near the source of instruction to allow the speaker to talk directly to the child to help reduce the interference of background noise. It is often necessary to experiment with different seating arrangements.

2. Get the student's full attention prior to giving instructions. It is often helpful to use a tactile prompt such as a pat on the hand, call the child's name, or establish eye contact in order to accomplish this.

3.   Reduce both auditory and visual distractions that might be competing for the child's attention. Other conversation and movement are the worst of these distractors. For independent work a study carrel, earmuffs, or both are helpful. Sometimes it is necessary to find a quiet space outside of the classroom.

4.   Speak distinctly, using as few words as possible; too much talking can distract the child.

5.   Simplify instruction by using simple one-step directions. Write down key words or assignments for students who can read. Information may need to be repeated or rephrased.

6.   Have the student reverbalize instruction, directions, or conversations. This not only helps the student remember what he heard but also gives the teacher a chance to see how the message was perceived. If it was incorrect, the message can be restated, and if correct, the student can be reinforced for good listening.

7.   Structure the environment as much as possible, using a consistent routine so the child knows what to expect at specific times.

8.   A buddy system can be helpful, especially for older students to check notes and assignments.

9.   Visual aids provide good reinforcement for the student with weak auditory skills. An overhead projector for lectures can be extremely helpful.

10.   Breaks during the day may be necessary for the child to relax. Tension can build and fatigue occur when children are constantly straining to attend and comprehend what is going on around them.

11.   Amplification systems that allow for direct input of the teacher's voice to the student without any additional sound (FM auditory training units) are helpful with students who have particular difficulty blocking out back-ground noise.

12.   It is most important to allow the student to experience as much success as possible to promote a good self-concept. When children are frustrated with themselves as well as having academic difficulties, it is hard to stimulate interest to build skills that will help restore confidence.

In addition to the above recommendations, it is often necessary for these students to receive small group or one to one instruction from a learning disabilities resource specialist. The severity of the disorder and the specific academic needs will determine the amount of time spent with the specialist. This time is best spent working in individualized reading, language, or math programs that replace regular classroom instruction or to provide additional skill building to maintain the child's performance in his classroom.

Once the central auditory processing disorder is diagnosed, it is helpful to simply explain to the child about his understanding skills. For young children this is often best done when situations that can be used as examples arise. For older students the explanation is quite simple, because they usually have experienced enough difficulties to understand the concept of central auditory processing. Caution must be taken so that the child does not use the central auditory processing problem as a crutch or an excuse for his or her behavior. To prevent this, it is important for the child, parent, and teacher to understand the responsibilities of each party in the management of the problem.

## At Home

The same recommendations that are given for school should be carried out at home. Again, a written list should be given the parents at the time the test results and recommendations are discussed. It is often difficult for parents to understand the central auditory processing concept. Whenever possible, therefore, they should be allowed to sit through the central auditory processing evaluation. This provides an opportunity to explain the tests to the parents as well as for the parents to see how their child performed during the assessment.

With subtle central auditory processing disorders, parents may not feel that problems exist in the home environment. This may be true, or it could be the response of a defensive parent. Always explain to the parents that their child's performance will vary depending upon the environment. At home the child may be secure in the established routine, whereas in a new situation, such as school, the child may respond quite differently. From year to year the child's performance will also vary. More problems are usually evident at the beginning of the school year as the child adjusts to a new teacher, new classroom, and new routine. As the child progresses gradewise, difficulties may also increase because the teaching styles generally move from concrete in thought and multisensory in presentation, to abstract and primarily verbal. Compensation skills are crucial for the child as the information to be learned reaches the lecture-style format.

## CONCLUSION

Children with central auditory processing disorders need an environment that is structured and consistent and shared with patient, loving adults who understand the needs of this special population. A good self-concept begins through this support at home and can be carried through the educational structure if time is taken to share the problem and recommendations with each new teacher. The child must also learn to deal with the effects of the central auditory processing problem so as to minimize their impact on educational achievement and performance and to maximize school success.

The past few years have seen real growth in interest and research in central auditory processing function in children. Although there is considerable controversy over diagnostic and remedial procedures, there is an accumulating body of research to provide us continually with a better understanding of this problem.

## REFERENCES

Bakker, D. Ear asymmetry with monaural stimulation: task influences. *Cortex*, 1969, *5*, 36–41.

Bakker, D., & deWit, J. Perceptual and cortical immaturity in developmental dyslexia. In L. Tarnopol & M. Tarnopol (Eds.), *Brain function and reading disabilities*. Baltimore: University Park Press, 1977.

Beasley, D. & Freeman, B. Time-altered speech as a measure of central auditory processing. In R. W. Keith (Ed.), *Central Auditory Dysfunction*. New York: Grune & Stratton, 1977.

Berlin, C. I., Hughes, L. F., Lowe-Bell, S. S., Berlin, H. L. Dichotic right ear advantage in chidren 5–13. *Cortex*, 1973, *9*, 372–402.

Birch, H. Functional effects of fetal malnutrition. *Hospital Practice*, 1971, 134–148.

Butler, K. Language processing disorders: factors in diagnosis and remediation. In R. Keith (Ed.), *Central auditory and language disorders in children*. Houston: College-Hill Press, 1981.

Clark, J. The effects of middle ear disease on speech and language development: a literature review. In R. Keith (Ed.), *Seminars in speech, language, hearing: auditory perceptual problems in children*. New York: Thieme-Stratton, 1980. Vol. 1 Chapter 6.

Cohen, R. Auditory skills and the communication process. In R. Keith (Ed.), *Seminars in speech, language and hearing: auditory perceptual problems in children* New York: Thieme-Stratton, 1980. Vol. 1 Chapter 2.

Colligan, R. Psychometric deficits related to perinatal stress. *Journal of Learning Disabilities*, 1974, *7*, 154–160.

DeConde, C., & McCarthy, J. Minimal auditory deficiency and its implications for learning. Unpublished Manuscript, 1980.

Federal Register, Department of Health, Education, and Welfare, Office of Education, Part III, December, 1977.

Flowers, A., & Costello, R. *Flowers-Costello Test of Central Auditory Abilities*. Dearborn, Mich.: Perceptual Learning Systems. 1970.

Gearheart, B., & Weishahn, M. *The handicapped child in the regular classroom*. St. Louis: C.V. Mosby, 1976.

Geschwind, N., & Levitsky, W. Human brain: Left-right asymmetries in temporal speech region. *Science*, 1968, *161*, 186–187.

Hammill, D. D., Larsen, S. C., Leigh, J., McNutt, G. A new definition of learning disabilities. *Learning Disability Quarterly*, 1981, *4*, 336–342.

Heasley, B. *Auditory perceptual disorders and remediation*. Springfield, Ill.: Charles C. Thomas, 1974.

Holm, V., & Kunze, L. Effect of chronic otitis media on language and speech development. *Pediatrics*, 1969, *43*, 833–838.

Ivey, R. G. *Tests of CNS auditory function.* Unpublished masters thesis, Colorado State University, Ft. Collins, Colorado, 1969.

Jerger, J. Speaks, C., Trammel, J. A new approach to speech audiometry. *Journal of Speech & Hearing Disorders*, 1968, *33*, 318–328.

Kaluger, G., & Kolson, C., *Reading and learning disabilities.* Columbus, Ohio: Charles E. Merrill, 1969.

Katz., J. The effects of conductive hearing loss on auditory function. *Asha*, 1978, *20*, 879–886.

Katz, J. *The Staggered Spondaic Word Test.* St. Louis, Mo: Auditec of St. Louis, 1973.

Keith, R. Tests of central auditory function. In R. Roesser & M. Downs (Eds.), *Auditory disorders in school children.* New York: Thieme-Stratton, 1981.

Knox, C., & Roesser, R. Cerebral dominance and auditory perceptual asymmetries in normal and dyslexic children. In R. Keith & J. Northern (Eds.), *Seminars in speech, language, hearing: auditory perceptual problems in children* New York: Thieme-Stratton, 1980. Chapter 9

Kottler, S. The identification and remediation of auditory problems. *Academic Therapy*, 1972, *8*,(1), 73–86.

Kurland, L., & Colodny, D. Psychiatric disability and learning problems. In L. Tarnopol (Ed.), *Learning disabilities: introduction to education and medical management.* Springfield, Ill.: Charles C. Thomas, 1969.

Lewis, N. Otitis media and linguistic incompetence. *Archives of Otolaryngology*, 1976, *102*, 387–390.

Needleman, A. The effects of hearing loss from early recurrent otitis media on speech and language development. In B. Jaffe (Ed.), *Hearing loss in children.* Baltimore: University Park Press, 1977.

Northern, J. & Downs, M. *Hearing in children* (2nd ed.). Baltimore: Williams & Wilkins, 1978.

Orton, S. Word blindness in school children. *Archives of Neurology Psychiatry* 1925, *14*, 581–585.

Pasamanick, B., & Knoblock, P. Brain damage and reproductive casualty. *American Journal of Orthopsychiatry*, 1960, *30*, 298–305.

Protti, E., Young, M., & Byrne, P. The evaluation of a child with auditory perceptual deficiencies: An interdisciplinary approach. In R. Keith and J. Northern (Eds.), *Seminars in speech, language, hearing: auditory perceptual problems in children.* (Vol. 1). New York: Thieme-Stratton, 1980. Chapt. 8

Rampp, D. Auditory perceptual disturbances. In A. Weston (Ed.), *Communicative disorders: an appraisal.* Springfield, Ill: Charles C. Thomas, 1972.

Rampp, D. *Auditory processing and learning disabilities.* Lincoln, Nebraska: Cliff Notes, 1980.

Reagan, C. *Handbook of auditory perceptual training.* Springfield, Ill: Charles C. Thomas, 1973.

Rees, N. Auditory processing factors in learning disorders: a view from Procrustes' bed. *Journal of Speech Disorders*, 1973, *38*, 304–315.

Rosenzweiz, M. Representation of the two ears at the auditory cortex. *American Journal of Physiology*, 1951, *167*, 147–158.

Speaks, C. Dichotic listening: a clinical or research tool? In M. Sullivan (Ed.), *Proceedings of a symposium on central auditory processing disorders.* Omaha, Nebraska: University of Nebraska Medical Center, 1975.

Tarnopol, L., & Tarnopol, M. Introduction to neuropsychology. In L. Tarnopol and M. Tarnopol (Eds.), *Brain function and reading disabilities.* Baltimore: University Park Press, 1977.

Tucker, J., Stevens, L., & Ysseldyke, J. Learning disabilities: the experts speak out. *Journal of Learning Disabilities*, 1983, *16*(1), 6–14.

Tunturi, A. A study on the pathway from the medial geniculate body to the acoustic cortex in the dog. *American Journal of Physiology*, 1946, *147*, 311–319.

Webster, D., & Webster, M. Effects of neonatal conductive hearing loss on brainstem auditory nuclei. *Archives of Otolaryngology*, 1977, *103*, 392–396.

Willeford, J. *Central Auditory Tests.* Unpublished material, Colorado State University, Fort Collins, Colorado.

Willeford, J., and Billger, J. *Ipsilateral-Contralateral Competing Sentence Test.* Unpublished material, Colorado State University, Fort Collins, Colorado.

Yule, W., & Rutter, M. Epidemiology and social implications of specific reading retardation. In R. Knights and D. Bakker (Eds.), *The neuropsychology of learning disorders: theoretical approaches.* Baltimore: University Park Press, 1976.

Zangwill, O. *Cerebral dominance and its relation to psychological function.* Edinburgh: Oliver & Boyd, 1960.

*J. Laurence Hayes*

# 11

# Interpreting in the K–12 Mainstream Setting

The intent of this chapter is to provide the reader with an overview of the interpreter in a mainstreaming (K–12) program with the hearing impaired. It considers the interpreter's role, function, training, and status in support service programming in the schools.

## DEFINITIONS

As with any profession, the field of interpreting has its own unique jargon. It seems beneficial to offer definitions of commonly used terms associated with the field in order to set the groundwork for further discussion.

INTERPRETER.   This is a generic term for an individual who functions as a communication link for hearing-impaired persons with hearing individuals. The formal distinction between interpreter and transliterator as used in the profession can be summarized as follows: an interpreter is the communication link who listens to spoken English

THE HEARING-IMPAIRED CHILD IN SCHOOL
ISBN 0-8089-1663-7

163

and communicates this via American Sign Language to the hearing-impaired person. The transliterator is the communication link who listens to spoken English and communicates this in a Signed English format. The interpreter also utilizes voice to communicate the hearing-impaired individual's American Sign Language to the hearing person. The same process applies to the transliterator who utilizes his voice to communicate Signed English from the hearing impaired to the hearing person.

SIGN LANGUAGE.   This is a generic term depicting the spectrum of visual "manual" communication utilized by and with hearing-impaired persons.

AMERICAN SIGN LANGUAGE (A.S.L.).   This visual gestural language possesses specific linguistic rules unlike English with particular sociolinguistic dynamics. American Sign Language is considered the "native" language of many hearing-impaired persons.

SIGNED ENGLISH.   Sign system(s) that have been designed to represent the English language. These systems follow English linguistical structure as closely as feasible. Included, but not limited to, these systems are Seeing Essential English (S.E.E.) and Linguistics of Visual English (L.O.V.E.).

PIDGIN SIGN ENGLISH (P.S.E.).   P.S.E. is a blend of manually-represented English with American Sign Language. As with a pidgin language, it is a combination of two separate languages, such as Border Spanish found in parts of the southwestern United States.

ORAL.   This refers to or describes a communication approach/methodology that does not involve a formal sign system. Rather, it involves speech reading, utilization of residual hearing, and speech "voice"production.

TOTAL COMMUNICATION.   Total Communication is a philosophical approach to communication with hearing-impaired individuals. This multifaceted approach utilizes all modes and methodologies of communication including oral, manual, and written forms. Most often, total communication is used by teachers in an educational setting for the enhancement of speech, language, and comprehension skills.

A representation of the communication modes employed by hearing-impaired individuals can best be diagrammed on a continuum. On the left is Oral, which does not include any form of sign language. This is English in all senses of the word; moving to the right, the next form is Signed English, then P.S.E. The final form on the right side is American Sign Language.

| Oral | Signed English | P.S.E. | A.S.L. |
|---|---|---|---|
| (Auditory Language Spoken English) | | Nonauditory Language-Visual Gestural) | |

The next step, Signed English is a type of sign language that represents English in a manual form. The influence and mixing of Signed English with A.S.L. produces a form of pidgin that is called Pidgin Sign English. It is of interest to note how many hearing individuals learn and acquire sign skills in the Signed English and P.S.E. range rather than A.S.L. Hearing-impaired individuals often know and utilize A.S.L. with other hearing-impaired individuals, but tend to utilize more P.S.E. or English with hearing signers. This may reflect sociolinguistic dynamics of the populations involved; however, this places the signing interpreter in a demanding situation as the communication link.

This is not a definitive continuum, and there is more in-depth research available. Those interested should pursue further readings and recognize this diagram as an introduction.

## THE ROLE OF THE INTERPRETER

On the surface, sign interpreting appears to be a mass of incongruous hand movements with assorted facial expressions and subtle body movements. In a practical sense, an interpreter is a two-way channel for information and communication. The expressive portion or interpreting is when interpreter "A" listens to speaker "B" and communicates this information to hearing-impaired person "C."

$$\begin{array}{c} \text{"C"} \\ \nearrow \\ \text{"A"} \longleftarrow \text{"B"} \end{array}$$

The receptive part of this communication is when the hearing-impaired person "C" signs, and interpreter "A" utilizes voice to represent auditorily the visual language to speaker "B."

$$\begin{array}{c} \text{"C"} \\ \swarrow \\ \text{"A"} \longrightarrow \text{"B"} \end{array}$$

This same basic flow chart can be applied to other one-on-one situations, classrooms, and lecture halls. Variations arise when considering physical placement of the interpreter, when utilizing more than one interpreter, or when there is need for separate oral, Signed English, or A.S.L. interpreters.

The physiological process involved is an area of which very little is known. It is relatively easy to observe the overt and tangible aspects of interpreting, but how this process occurs deals with neurological functions of the brain and related muscle coordination/control. This in itself may seem almost magical to the untrained observer, but underlying is a complex process to which we can only make generalizations.

## The Signing Interpreter-Transliterator

The first signing interpreter to be explained will be the Signed English interpreter or transliterator—the person working in only one language, English.

In the most basic expressive sense, the transliterator must first listen to the verbal message, mentally pair it with a sign that represents the English word, and physically produce it. The transliterator mouths the words without projecting voice, produces appropriate facial expression/body posture, while, simultaneously assimilating new information. For an example of the complexity of the interpretor's job, many lectures are delivered at 130–160 words per minute. The receptive aspect requires the transliterator to read the signs visually (100 plus signs per minute), pair an English word with the image, and verbally produce the word. Again, the transliterator must be aware of facial expression and subtle body movements of the hearing-impaired person and take these into account. These must be considered as part of the total message—shaping the voice inflection and intonation of the transliterator.

## The Interpreter

Similar rules apply to the interpreter, although there are several important differences. The interpreter works two separate languages—English and American Sign Language. When listening to the spoken message, the interpreter must understand the meaning; encode this with appropriate sign(s), facial expression, and body language; and physically produce it. Mouth "movements" are an important part of interpreting, these are shapes correlated with facial expressions and signs. This is not mouthing in the transliterator mode, since it would be impossible to mouth English while signing American Sign Language. They are changing languages, employing the dynamics particular to two separate languages and their sociolinguistic differences. Many spoken languages will not interpret verbatim to another language without losing specific meaning and intent. In numerous cases, a literal translation will result in an absurd statement. Both these aspects apply to English and American Sign Language. For instance, if someone literally signed: "He drove me up the wall," to an A.S.L. signing hearing-impaired individual in Signed English, it would appear silly, at best.

## The Oral Interpreter

Oral interpreting is a relatively new realm of support service for hearing-impaired persons. The oral interpreter serves in much the same capacity—linking communication—as does the signing interpreter. Simple mouthing of words is not at all sufficient for assuming the role of an oral interpreter, much more is involved. Consider where throat and mouth sounds are formulated, the shape of the lips, and the location of the tongue for various words. How visible is the word green compared with the word red on an individual's lips? When words have similar sounds or appearances, others can be substituted by the interpreter i.e., wear and where, in order to clarify the speaker's sentence. Selection of appropriate words for their visibility and meaning combined with a keen use of facial expression make the oral interpreter's task an involved one. While the oral interpreter does not use formal signs, he may combine subtle natural gestures. A raised palm, pointing with the right or left hand to show location of an objective, all may be incorpated as a natural gesture.

A final and important point related to the physiological aspects of interpreting is that not all signing interpreters are appropriate for all signing hearing-impaired individuals. The same basic rule applies to oral interpreters and oral hearing-impaired individuals. This may seem obvious. However, facial features, left handed and right handed signing, and other factors must all be given due consideration by those involved.

## ENVIRONMENTAL CONSIDERATIONS

The environment in which the interpreter works can either facilitate communication or bring it to a standstill. Consider the position of the speaker, hearing-impaired person, and the interpreter. For example, in a lecture situation the interpreter should be positioned between the hearing-impaired person and the speaker.

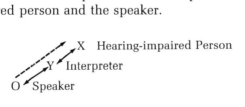

This allows the hearing-impaired person to view the speaker through peripheral vision while watching the interpreter. Being able to compare the intent/feeling portrayed by the interpreter with those of the speaker gives a more complete picture. Should the speaker utilize a chalkboard or other visual aids, this positioning provides immediate access. In an interview or other type of one-on-one situation the interpreter should be positioned next to the speaker as diagrammed below.

Lighting, clothing, jewelry, and make-up are all part of the environment and must be taken into account. These interpreting considerations are basic in nature, and a detailed explanation of all potential situations is beyond the scope of this chapter. For further information on this aspect of interpreting, the reader can consult the following books for in-depth information: (1) *Introduction to Interpreting for Interpretors/Transliterators, Hearing Impaired Consumers, Hearing Consumers* by Dirst, Caccamise, DeBries et al and (2) *Sign Language Interpreter—A Basic Resource Book* by Solow.

## FUNCTION OF THE INTERPRETER IN THE SCHOOL

The profession of interpreting is a relatively new development, and the introduction of the interpreter into the public school system is truly in its infancy. There is much to be learned about the various communication modes utilized by the interpreter, be they manual or oral. One thing that can safely be stated is that there truly is a need for professional interpreting services throughout our educational systems. Earlier in this chapter, the flow of information through the interpreter was diagrammed and discussed as a two-way system; that is, the interpreter is present and working for both the speaker and the hearing-impaired individual. Within the mainstreamed educational setting, this two-way access provided by the interpreter should not be limited to the classroom, but should also include nonacademic school functions. School assemblies and sporting events can all be considered an integral part of a hearing-impaired person's socialization. As these and other events round out a hearing person's personality development, they are also a critical part of the mainstreamed individual's total education.

The role of the interpreter in the classroom should be one of a communication facilitator. The interpreter may be called upon to fulfill roles outside his or her realm of training due to ease of communication with the hearing-impaired person. This is unfortunate, because interpreters are not trained as teachers, counselors, or supervisors; it is considered an unfair shift of responsibility to expect this performance. When an interpreter is brought into the educational setting, a clear distinction of responsibilities should be outlined by all those involved. Performing other related tasks to supplement the instructional process (not to replace those involved with instruction) may be realistic. Performing nonacademic related tasks may be requested and necessary. However, conflict of role/interest must always be taken into consideration for maximum effectiveness.

Skill or proficiency of the interpreter is extremely difficult to determine by those unfamiliar with the field, unless there is outside evaluation available. This outside criteria may be based upon state or national interpreter evaluation systems, and in some instances, upon other professional interpreters.

Relevant to evaluation and skill level of interpreters is the distinction between an interpreter and a signer. Two or three sign language classes do not make an interpreter. Consider the length of time required to become proficient in German, French, or Italian. Now one must ask, "How many additional years would be required to become a proficient interpreter of that language?" A minimum of 3 to 4 years of training is required to prepare an entry-level interpreter. This is a conservative estimate, and many professional interpreter trainers could easily justify the addition of 2 to 3 years to this estimate. American Sign language has endured the stigma of being considered an unstructured group of hand movements, easily learned in a few weeks or months. This belief can sometimes be wrongly reflected in selection criteria for interpreters by educational programs, and can be compared to providing half a wheelchair ramp.

Finding qualified interpreters is not always an easy task. There are several ways to approach this problem. The following list offers several ideas:

1. local or state Registry of Interpreters for the Deaf organization
2. National Registry of Interpreters for the Deaf organization
3. local or state organizations of the deaf
4. local or state agencies/organization's educational programs serving the deaf
5. colleges or universities that offer Interpreter Training Programs.

Selection and utilization of an interpreter is probably the most critical aspect of education programming for some hearing-impaired students. Without this link or with improper use, all other aspects of education/socialization will not be properly availed to these persons.

## CONCLUSION

Flow of communication through the interpreter is a two-way avenue that opens all aspects of the educational process for the hearing-impaired person.

Special consideration should be given to the function and role of the interpreter in the educational system to ensure proper utilization of their training and skills. Directly related to function is the proficiency level of the interpreter and subsequent selection criteria. Locating qualified interpreters may prove to be the most difficult problem facing hearing-impaired individuals or the educational system that wishes to hire them.

The integral physiological work done by the interpreter will be better understood as research further unfolds the process involved. A more comprehensive understanding of the diversified components found in interpreting will help those involved in training, educational planning, and most importantly, the student.

Interpreting is a critical component in linking the hearing-impaired and hearing worlds for the mutual benefit of education and social growth. It is towards this goal that the educational interpreter strives on a daily and professional basis.

## SELECTED READINGS

Babbini, B. The component skills of interpreting as viewed by interpreters. *Journal of Rehabilitation of the Deaf*, 1974, 7, 20–27.

Baker, C., and Cokely, D. *American sign language: a teacher's resource text on grammar and culture*. Silver Spring, Maryland: T. J. Publishers, 1980.

Bellugi, U., and Klima, E. *The Signs of Language*. Cambridge, Massachusetts: Harvard University Press, 1979.

Cokely, D. Sign language interpreters: a demographic survey. *Journal of Sign Language Studies*, 1981, 32, 261–286.

Dickens, L. *Facilitating manual communication for teachers, students, and interpreters*. Silver Spring, Maryland: Registry of Interpreters for the Deaf, Inc., 1978.

Dirst, R., Caccamise, F., DeVries D. R., et al. (Eds.). *Introduction to interpreting for interpreters/transliterators, hearing impaired consumers, hearing consumers*. Silver Spring, Maryland: Registry of Interpreters for the Deaf, Inc.

Markowicz, H. *American sign language: fact and fancy*. Washington, D.C.: Public Service Programs, Gallaudet College, 1977.

Moores, D. *Educating the deaf—psychology, principles and practices*. Boston: Houghton Mifflin, 1978.

Northcott, W. The oral interpreter: a necessary support specialist for the hearing impaired. *Volta Review*, 1977, 77, 136–144.

Solow, S. N. *Sign language interpreting—a basic resource book*. Silver Spring, Maryland: National Association of the Deaf, 1981.

Woodward, J. *How you gonna get to heaven if you can't talk with Jesus: on depathologizing deafness*. Silver Spring, Maryland: T.J. Publishers, 1982.

*Rhonda E. Kaley*

# 12

# Responses to Questions by Teachers and Parents about Hearing Impairment

Parents and educators frequently raise questions about the cause of hearing loss and its effects on a child's development. This chapter will review three areas of concern that are most commonly raised by them: (1) deafness and hereditary causes, (2) methods of communication by the hearing impaired, and (3) the effects of noise on hearing. Although the areas may seem unrelated, each is important in terms of their effect on children, and the questions of their parents and teachers.

## HEREDITARY DEAFNESS

Hereditary childhood hearing losses are typically bilateral, severe to profound, and sensorineural in nature (Kinney, 1950; Northern and Downs, 1978). Konigsmark's (1969) review identified approximately 70 known types of hereditary deafness in humans. Hereditary losses are classified as congenital, that is, present at the time of birth. However, not all congenital hearing losses are hereditary. Other prenatal causes include viral infections, drug ingestion by the mother, Rh factor, and birth injuries. This section will look only at those losses transmitted through genetic defects.

## How Is Hereditary Deafness Transmitted?

Hereditary hearing losses can be either dominant (10 percent) or recessive (90 percent). In order to have dominant transmission, either one parent or both parents carry the affected gene. If only one parent carries the abnormal gene, about 50 percent of the offspring will be affected. If both parents carry the same affected gene, all of the offspring will be affected. It is important to remember that the genetic code for hearing loss may be carried by more than one gene. Therefore, if both parents are affected, but by different genetic codes, the incidence of hearing loss in the offspring may not be 100 percent.

If the hearing loss is recessive, both parents must be carriers of the same defective genetic code. Following the rules of genetic transmission, only 25 percent of the offspring will be affected, and 50 percent will be carriers. Because both parents must carry the abnormal genetic code, consanguineous marriages may produce a higher incidence of hearing loss (English and Sargent, 1982).

## How Are Hereditary Hearing Losses Diagnosed?

The key factor in diagnosing dominant hereditary transmission is a family history of hearing loss. Since one or both parents are affected, it is usually an easy task to trace back the pattern of inheritance. Identification of recessive transmission is more difficult, since the parents are only carriers of the trait and are unaffected. Often recessive traits can never be proven to the satisfaction of the diagnostician.

## What Is A Syndrome?

In some cases, hereditary hearing loss is part of a *syndrome*. A syndrome is a collection of multiple congenital malformations. Some of the more common syndromes with associated hearing loss are Alport's, Crouzon's, Downs, Pierre Robin, Pendred's, and Treacher Collins (Northern and Downs, 1978). In some syndrome conditions, the hearing loss may be progressive and worsen as the child gets older.

## How Can Parents Learn More About the Possibility of Future Offspring Being Affected?

Once parents have learned that their child is deaf due to hereditary factors, they often express concern about the effect the factors will have on their future children. Genetic counseling may be useful in helping parents deal with the realities of hereditary transmission.

Stewart (1973) has identified the steps of genetic counseling, which include: (1) a complete family, pregnancy, birth, and infancy history; (2) physical examinations of the affected child and other family members; and (3) laboratory work as required. Parents and other family members then attend counseling sessions to learn more about the problems and the risks involved in future pregnancies.

One of the problems that must frequently be dealt with in counseling is feelings of guilt, particularly when one parent is identified as the carrier of the defective genetic code. Obviously, the parent will feel the weight of the guilt, and effective counseling may help in the acknowledgment of that emotion and in providing ways to deal with it (Northern and Downs, 1978).

Genetic counselors often find it useful to develop family trees or pedigrees to determine the mode of inheritance (Northern and Downs, 1978). By tracing back through the family structure, it may be possible to identify the gene as dominant, recessive, or sex-linked. Such information can be useful to parents in terms of family planning.

Genetic counseling can only provide "risk" information. Parents must still accept the responsibility for decision making. But by providing information, counseling can help parents make informed decisions.

## METHODS OF COMMUNICATION

There are three philosophies of communication currently advocated by educators and other professionals who work with hearing-impaired children. Methods of communication most often discussed include (1.) Oralism, (2.) Manual Communication, and (3.) Total Communication. Studies of language development and educational achievement of hearing-impaired children seem to indicate that there is no "right" method. Instead, the system selected must meet the communicative needs of each individual child. Oralism seems to be the predominant method for the education of hearing-impaired children. Silverman and Lane (1970), for example, reported that at that time 85 percent of children attending schools for the deaf were being taught by an oral method.

This section of Chapter 12 will look at each of the three philosophies and examine the benefits and limitations of each.

### What is Oralism?

The oral approach usually involves the combined use of auditory and visual information. The visual mode is limited to speech reading, and sign language and gestures are excluded. Although there are several methods of teaching oral communication, they are not always distinguishable.

Generally, to succeed with an oral approach hearing-impaired children should have some residual hearing in order to utilize auditory information to the maximum extent. The use of some type of amplification system is usually recommended.

Among the strongest advocates of oralism are the parents of the hearing-impaired children. Parents are hesitant to utilize a communication system that would make their child seem "different" from other children. The parents feel that if their child is oral, their child will be more readily accepted in the hearing world. Although such feelings are natural, parents must realize that there are numerous instances when the oral approch may not be successful. Opponents of the oral approach cite many reasons why the method may not meet the expectations of parents or educators. The major complaints center around the use of speech reading as a means of speech reception (Northern and Downs, 1978). Lip reading requires a combination of good visual skills, adequate lighting, and a limited distance between the speaker and "listener." Even under the best of conditions, the ability to speech read is not developed in all children.

Another problem with speech reading often cited is that it is too ambiguous. Northern and Downs (1978) state that the ambiguity is the result of three inter-related factors. The first is that many sounds and words appear to be identical when viewed on the lips. These visually similar sounds are called *homophenous sounds*, such as /p, b, m/. In other words it is difficult to visually distinguish between them. Second, many sounds are not readily visible when produced. For example, sounds produced in the back of the throat, such as /k, ng, and g/, are difficult to view by looking at the face and must be perceived auditorily to distinguish them. Finally, the speakers themselves may speak indistinctly, making it difficult to visually perceive the sounds and words they are uttering.

Problems such as these seem to indicate that oralism in isolation is not always the method of choice in the teaching profoundly hearing-impaired children. But the limitations are not so extreme with children having lesser degrees of hearing loss. Generally, oralism would be the method of choice for mildly and moderately hearing-impaired children who have more usable residual hearing.

## What Is Manualism?

If oralism is not the method of choice, what are the alternatives? One alternative to oralism is manual communication, often referred to as *sign language*. Manual communication utilizes a strictly visual approach to language with no auditory input. As there are advocates for oralism in teaching language to hearing-impaired children, there are also advocates for manualism, particularly for the more profoundly hearing impaired. For example, Garretson (1963) advocates the use of sign language and cites four assets of manual communication for use with hearing-impaired children:

1. the elimination of anxiety and stress that can be created by denying children the right to use their hands to communicate when speech has not been developed.
2. the elimination of doubt as to what is being communicated, thus easing frustrations
3. the clarity of using the larger hand movements rather than relying on small or nonvisual lip movements
4. the lack of discrimination against hearing-impaired children and the opportunity to participate and learn from classroom activities.

Garretson concludes that since manual systems have persisted among deaf adults and seem to be the preferred method of communication by the majority of the deaf, there must be some value to the sign language method.

*Are There Different Sign Systems?*

Currently, there are several sign systems in use throughout the United States. American Sign Language (ASL) has existed for over 100 years and combines signs, finger spelling, and facial and body language. ASL is the sign system used by most deaf adults, since the development of other sign systems has been relatively recent. American Sign Language, as opposed to the newer systems, is a language apart from the English language system. Davis and Hardick (1981) cite several distinctions between ASL and spoken English. First, not all ASL signs can be readily translated into English words. Many signs represent a concept as opposed to a single word. Second, ASL uses body language or gestures to represent pronouns, modifiers, and other function words, when no sign exists for the particular word. Third, the rate of signing can indicate stress of emphasis and may also change the meaning of a particular sign. Finally, repetition of a sign may pluralize a word or completely change its meaning. For example, if the sign for "again" is repeated two or three times it becomes "often."

American Sign Language does not conform to English syntax, and it is impossible to sign in ASL and concurrently speak what is being signed using strict spoken English form (Davis & Hardick, 1981). ASL is considered a foreign language by many. In fact, some universities are allowing students to take such forms of sign language to meet their foreign language requirements.

Because of the structural language problems of American Sign Language, newer sign systems have been developed to better represent spoken English. The concept behind these forms is to have deaf children see English in the same form that hearing children hear English, thereby providing a more natural learning environment (Davis & Hardick, 1981).

One of the first manual English systems to be developed was Seeing Essential English (SEE[1]). Developed by Anthony (1971), SEE[1] uses the same English word order found in spoken English, with signs representing both word forms and word parts, including suffixes and prefixes. SEE[1] has incorporated many ASL signs into its language. New signs were also developed, however, making SEE[1] the system with the largest vocabulary (Northern and Downs, 1978).

Signing Exact English (SEE[2]) was developed in 1972 by Gustason, Pfetzing, and Zawolkow (1972), who were also involved in the group that developed SEE[1]. Because of the complexities of SEE[1], it was felt that a simpler system was needed. SEE[2] utilizes a one-word, one-sign system and eliminates much of the root word utilization seen in SEE[1].

A third system, Signed English, was developed by Bornstein and others at Gallaudet College (Kannapell, Hamilton, and Bornstein, 1969). Signed English utilizes American Sign Language words in an English syntax structure (Northern & Downs, 1978). The system also utilizes signed markers to represent pluralization, verb tense, possessive forms, and other English morphological forms.

Sign systems are being accepted more and more both in the early language training and later education of hearing-impaired children. Studies are being conducted to look at the educational implications of the use of various sign systems; however, at the present time, no decision has been reached as to which system is best.

### What is Total Communication?

Brill (1976) defines total communication as "a philosophy requiring the incorporation of appropriate aural, manual, and oral modes of communication in order to ensure effective communication with and among hearing-impaired persons" (p. 358). Basically, total communication utilizes every form of input available to present vocabulary and language concepts to hearing-impaired children (Northern & Downs, 1978). The use of total communication would allow hearing-impaired children to use whatever sensory or language system is most appropriate for their individual needs and not be constrained within the limitations of just one system.

Total communication has seen a tremendous growth in acceptance among educators. A study completed in 1976 (Jordan, Gustason, and Rosen, 1976) showed that of 343 programs for deaf children surveyed, 302 had changed from oral/aural methods and 333 of the progrms had changed to total communication, while only eight programs had changed from total communication to another system. Although there remains some opposition to the use of total communication, the results above indicate a definite trend toward the use of it in the education of hearing-impaired children.

## How Is The Method of Communication Chosen?

As mentioned before, there is no "right" method of communication. There seems to be a prevailing trend to start all hearing impaired in an oral program and to continue with that emphasis as long as the child is successful. The problem arises, however, in determining just how successful the child really is. More professionals are now looking to total communication in order to answer the question of the method of choice.

## NOISE-INDUCED HEARING LOSSES

Earlier in this chapter we discussed congenital hereditary types of hearing losses. Although there are some exceptions, most hereditary hearing losses are present at birth. In this section we will look at one type of acquired hearing loss—noise-induced hearing loss. Exposure to excessive noise is the most frequent cause of acquired hearing loss in the United States. As levels of noise increase as well as avenues to exposure to excessive noise, the topic is extremely relevant for parents and educators. There is much research available that has concentrated on the harmful effects of noise exposure on an industrial population. Limited research is available, however, on the effects of noise on children.

## What Is A Noise-Induced Hearing Loss?

Miller (1974) states that a hearing loss may result from exposure to noise of sufficient intensity on a sufficient number of occasions or for a sufficient duration. Although the hearing loss may only be temporary, in some cases the exposure can cause a permanent, irreversible hearing loss. Noise-induced hearing loss is usually gradual, and a person may suffer significant damage to the inner ear mechanism before any effects of the loss are noticed. Hearing losses resulting from excessive noise exposure are cochlear in nature, and typically occur in the frequency range initially around 4000Hz. When first exposed to intense noise, a person may notice a decrease in their ability to hear following the exposure. This phenomenon is known as *temporary threshold shift* and is caused by "fatigue" of the nerve cells in the cochlea (Newby, 1979). After a period of time, the hearing will recover to pre-exposure level. If exposure continues for extended periods of time, the damage can become permanent. Continued exposure will result in further decrease in hearing acuity over time.

Another type of hearing loss resulting from noise exposure is called *acoustic trauma*. Acoustic trauma is a sudden loss of hearing acuity resulting from a single, sudden, intense sound exposure, such as an explosion, which can cause structural damage to the hearing mechanism. In the case of children, probably the most common cause of acoustic trauma is firecrackers (Ward and Glorig, 1961).

## What Are The Major Causes of Noise-Induced Hearing Loss In Children?

Among the reported possible causes of noise-induced hearing loss in children are snowmobiles (Bess and Poynor, 1972, 1974); model airplane engines tested indoors (Bess and Powell, 1972); real and toy firearms (Hodge and McCommons, 1966; Marshall and Brandt, 1974); farm machinery (see Weber, McGovern, and Zink, 1967); and firecrackers (Ward and Glorig, 1961). In addition, Ruckelshaus (1972) presented some evidence that acoustic impulses of toy caps may also cause damage to the hearing mechanism.

More recent areas of concern are exposure to loud music and shop-noise in the high schools. Woodford and O'Farrell (1983) collected data on sound levels in school shops and their effects on students' hearing levels. The results from this comprehensive study revealed that sound levels in many school-related activities were sufficient to provide a potential hazard to hearing and that those students who were involved in the high sound level activities were more apt to have high-frequency hearing losses than the students who were not involved in those activities. They also found that the use of firearms might be a contributing factor in the loss of hearing acuity.

Roeser (1980) cited a survey completed in two high school woodworking shop areas that found that more than two-thirds of the equipment in use had noise levels in excess of 90dBA, which is the minimum excessive noise level for industrial workers.

Parents often express concern about the loudness of the music to which their children are exposed—or to which they expose themselves. Exposure to loud music can come from at least three sources: (1) live rock concerts, (2) recorded music (discotheque), and (3) music listened to through earphones. Lebo and Oliphant (1969) suspected that the hearing acuity of teenagers who were exposed to loud music was being affected. More recent studies have presented contradictory results about the actual danger of loud music exposure, however, most studies conclude that there is a risk of temporary hearing loss even if no permanent damage occurs.

A study by Rintlemann and Borus (1968) found that only 5 percent of the rock musicians studied had developed noise-induced hearing losses. A later study by Jerger and Jerger (1970) reported temporary threshold shifts of over 15dB in eight of the nine rock musicians evaluated. Rintlemann (1977), in a longitudinal study of the hearing of rock musicians, found no noise-induced hearing loss associated with exposure to the music over a period of 5–10 years. Axelsson and Lindgren (1978) found that temporary threshold shifts were more pronounced in audience listeners than in the musicians themselves, and males showed more threshold shift than females. Axelsson and Lindgren (1978) concluded that exposure to live rock music at 100dBA for 2 hours is the limit of exposure to avoid the risk of permanent damage to hearing. A probable reason for this lack of permanent damage is that there are adequate periods of time for temporary hearing losses to recover between times of exposure.

Axelsson and Lindgren (1981) reported an average sound level of 95dBA for recorded discotheque music. The data suggested, however, that "a normal exposure to pop music" for the audience—that is, one or two visits each month for a couple of hours—would "hardly imply a risk of permanent damage in the exposed listener" (p. 68).

Portable stereo radio-cassette players are becoming popular throughout the country. Katz and associates (1982) reported sound levels for three brands of recorders. The volume controls ranged from one to ten, and at a setting of four, sound levels of 93–108dB were reported. Sound levels of 115dB + are found at a volume setting of eight. Dr. Jane Madell (1983), the director of the New York League for the Hard of Hearing, reported findings on how high consumers were actually playing the portable stereos. Using a calibrated sound level meter, Dr. Madell randomly sampled persons using the recorders on a New York street and found virtually all the recorders were being played at levels above 100dB, and some were close to 120dB. These levels can be damaging to the hearing mechanism, and Dr. Madell suggested that the consumers should be warned of the risks involved.

## What Can Be Done to Avoid the Risk of Hearing Loss in Children and Teenagers?

The following suggestions might help avoid the risks of permanent hearing loss:

1. avoid high music exposure levels—if you have to yell to be heard above the noise, the sound level is dangerously high (Lipscomb, 1983)
2. use ear protectors (plugs or muffs) when in noisy environments
3. eliminate or reduce unnecessary noise over which you have some control (Lipscomb, 1983)—turn down the stereos to a level where you can hear someone talking to you at a normal conversation level
4. take a rest period away from the noise whenever possible. Parents, educators, and children alike should be aware of the problems caused by excessive noise exposure and do everything possible to avoid the effects.

## REFERENCES

Anthony, D.A. & Associates. *Seeing Essential English manual.* Anaheim, Ca.: Educational Services Division, Anaheim Union High School District, 1971.

Axelsson, A., & Lindgren, F. Pop music and hearing. *Ear and Hearing,* 1981, *2*, 64–69.

Axelsson, A., & Lindgren, F. Temporary threshold shifts after exposure to pop music. *Scandanavian Audiology,* 1978, *7*, 127–135.

Bess, F. H., & Powell, R.L. Hearing hazard from model airplanes. *Clinical Pediatrics,* 1972, *11*, 621–624.

Bess, F. H., & Poynor, R.E. Snowmobile engine noise and hearing. *Archives of Otolaryngology,* 1972, *95*, 164–168.

Brill, R.G. Definition of total communication. *American Annals of the Deaf,* 1976, *121*, 358.

Davis, J.M., & Hardick, E.J. *Rehabilitative audiology for children and adults.* New York: John Wiley & Sons, 1981.

English, G.M., & Sargent, R.S. Medical and surgical treatment of hearing loss. In M.J. Lass, L.V. McReynolds, J.L. Northern, & D.E. Yoder (Eds.), *Speech language and hearing* (Vol. 3). Philadelphia: W.B. Saunders, 1982.

Garretson, M.D. The need for multiple communication skills in the education process of the deaf. *Rocky Mountain Leader,* 1963, *62*, 1–8.

Gustason, G., Pfetzing, D., & Zawolkow, E. *Signing Exact English.* Rossmoor, Ca: Modern Signs Press, 1972.

Hodge, D.C., & McCommons, B.M. Acoustical hazards of children's toys. *Journal of the Acoustical Society of America,* 1966, *40*, 911.

Jerger, J., & Jerger, S. Temporary threshold shift in rock-and-roll musicians. *Journal of Speech and Hearing Research,* 1970, *13*, 218–224.

Jordan, I., Gustason, G., & Rosen, R. Current communication trends at programs for the deaf. *American Annals of the Deaf,* 1976, *121*, 527–532.

Kannapell, B., Hamilton, L., & Bornstein, H. *Signs for instructional purposes.* Washington, D.C.: Gallaudet College Press, 1969.

Katz, A., Gerstman, H., Sanderson, R., & Buchanan, R. Stereo earphones and hearing loss. *New England Journal of Medicine*, 1982, *307*, 1460–1461.

Kinney, C.E. Pathology of hereditary deafness. *Annals of Otology, Rhinology and Laryngology*, 1950, *59*, 1117–1122.

Konigsmark, B.W. Hereditary deafness in man. *New England Journal of Medicine*, 1969, *281*, 713–720; 774–778; 827–832.

Lebo, C.P., & Oliphant, K.P. Music as a source of acoustic trauma. *Laryngoscope*, 1969, *78*, 1211–1218.

Lipscomb, D.M. The other side of tinnitus. *American Tinnitus Association Newsletter*, 1983, *8*, 1–2.

Madell, J.R. Newsletter: The Suzanne Pathy Speak-Up Institute, Inc. 1983, *5*, 3.

Marshall, L., & Brandt, J. Temporary threshold shift from a toy cap gun. *Journal of Speech and Hearing Disorders*, 1974, *39*, 163–168.

Miller, J.D. Effects of noise on people. *Journal of the Acoustical Society of America*, 1974, *56*, 729–764.

Newby, H.A. *Audiology* (4th ed.). Englewood Cliffs, N.J.: Prentice-Hall, 1979.

Northern, J., & Downs, M. *Hearing in children*. Baltimore: Williams & Wilkins, 1978.

Rintelmann, W. Paper presented at Medical Audiology Workshop. Vail, Colorado, 1977.

Rintelmann, W.F., & Borus, J. Noise-induced hearing loss and rock and roll music. *Archives of Otolaryngology*, 1968, *88*, 57–65.

Roeser, R. J. Industrial hearing conservation programs in the high schools (Protect the ear before the 12th year). *Ear and Hearing*, 1980, *1*, 119–120.

Ruckelshaus, W. Report to the President and Congress on noise. Rep. Admin. EPA, *U.S. Senate Document #92-163*, Chapter 1, 1972, pp. 38–39.

Silverman, S.R., & Lane, H.S. Deaf Children. In H. Davis & S.R. Silverman (Eds.), *Hearing and deafness* (3rd ed.). New York: Holt, Rhinehart & Winston, 1970.

Stewart, J.M. Genetic counseling. In J. Clausen, M. Flook, B. Ford, M. Green, and E. Popiel (Eds.), *Maternity nursing today*. New York: McGraw-Hill, 1973.

Ward, W.D., & Glorig, A. A case of firecrackers-induced hearing loss. *Laryngoscope*, 1961, *71*, 1590–1596.

Weber, H., McGovern, F., & Zink, D. An evaluation of 1000 children with hearing loss. *Journal of Speech and Hearing Disorders*, 1967, *32*, 343–354.

Woodford, C., & O'Farrell, M.L. High-frequency loss of hearing in secondary school students: an investigation of possible etiologic factors. *Language, Speech, and Hearing Services in Schools*, 1983, *14*, 22–28.

*Karen L. Dilka*

# 13

# Resource Materials for Use with Hearing-Impaired Children in School and at Home

The following lists of materials are suggested for specific use with the hearing impaired.* The range of materials is limited to the exclusive areas of speech and language, due to the basic scope of this book. Three educational levels have been established to organize the content. It must be recognized, however, that many of these materials can be utilized for more than one level. Therefore, they have been classified according to their entry level of use.

These listings do not encompass the array of materials available or all the names of publishing companies producing such materials. Other resources, materials, and details may be obtained through the publishing companies, various schools for the hearing impaired, and the reference book *Curriculum Materials Useful for the Hearing Impaired* (McCarr and Wisser, 1979).

---

*A publisher's reference list that lists in alphabetical order the names of the publishers of the materials described in this chapter is found at the conclusion of the chapter.

THE HEARING-IMPAIRED CHILD IN SCHOOL
ISBN 0-8089-1663-7

## PRESCHOOL LISTINGS

### American Guidance Service

Peabody Early Experiences Kit
Builds cognitive, social, and linguistic skills.

Peabody Language Development Kit, Level P
Encourages development of oral language and cognitive skills.

Small Wonder, Level 2
18–36 months, remedially to 5 years. Teaches children about themselves, others, their surroundings, and the world through language development activities.

### Bowman/Noble Publishers, Inc.

Early Childhood Education Series
Part I—About Myself
Part II—The World Around Me
Part III—I Talk–I Think–I Reason

Project Me
How Are You Feeling Today?
If You Do Something
I Know How You Feel
Body Image—Level I
Body Image—Level II
Let's Look For Things
Moving Day
Directionality Program
Get Ready to Read and Write
Visual Guessing Games
Try This For Size and Shape
(69 Filmstrips and Cassettes)

### Developmental Learning Materials (DLM)

DLM produces additional materials useful in the classroom that are not listed due to the obvious space limit. Similar materials may also be purchased from other companies.
Association Picture Cards, I, II, III
Body Concept Spirit Masters I and II
Building Match-ups
Category Cards
Colored Inch Cubes
Colored Inch Cube Designs
Halves to Wholes

Large Parquetry Blocks
Large Parquetry Designs
Multivariant Sequencing Bead Patterns
Multivariant Sequencing Beads
Peg Boards
Peg Board Designs
Sequential Picture Cards II
Small Parquetry Blocks
Small Parquetry Designs I, II, III
Puzzles
Animal Puzzles
Dimensional Puzzle
Form Puzzle
Job Puzzles
Large Body Puzzles
People Puzzles-Families
Perception Puzzle
Shapes Puzzles
Size and Shape Puzzle

### Ideal School Supply Company

Form-A-Sound
Instructs students in basic phonetics: consonant sounds, long and short vowel sounds, and digraphs.

Puppet Enrichment Program
Stimulates language development and listening skills. Four puppets with detaching interchangeable parts

### Instructs/McGraw-Hill

The Classification Game
Discovering Opposites Cards
Let's Learn Sequence
My Face and Body Felt Cutouts
We Dress for the Weather Felt Cutouts
When I Grow Up I Want To Be . . . Felt Figures
Where Do They Belong? Animal Classification

### Mafex Associates, Inc.

Talk! Talk! Talk!

A testing-teaching language program according to a developmental sequence.

### Modern Education Corporation
Picture Sequence Cards
Places and Things Pictures and Names
Speech Lingo (speech sounds)
Spin It (speech sounds)

### Society For Visual Education
A variety of visually stimulating materials. Examples include:
Thanksgiving for King
Animal Mothers and Babies (with cassette)
Animals in the Zoo (with cassette)
Animals on the Farm (with cassette)
Animals in the City (with cassette)
The Hare and the Tortoise (with cassette)
The Thanksgiving Story
The Christmas Donkey
The Baby King
Rudolph the Red Nose Reindeer
Rudolph Shines Again
The Fir Tree
The Little Engine that Could
The Elves and the Shoemaker
Night Before Christmas
Jack and the Beanstalk
Tale of Peter Rabbit
Mary Had a Little Lamb
The Ugly Duckling
Snow White and the Seven Dwarfs
The Little Pine Tree
The Little Red Hen
Rackety Rabbit
Town Mouse and Country Mouse
Paddy's Christmas
Twinkle Twinkle
Copy Kitten
Little Bobo and His Blue Jacket
Fuss Bunny
So Long
Our Auto Trip
Hide Away Puppy
Chester the Little Pony
Happy Mother's Day
Happiest Easter
Johnny the Fireman

Valentines Mean You Care
Mother Goose I
Mother Goose II
Mother Goose III
Hansel and Gretel I and II
The Three Billy Goats Gruff
Little Red Riding Hood
The Three Little Pigs
The Gingerbread Boy
The Bunnies Easter Surprise

## St. Johns School For the Deaf

Speech Books for the Deaf
  My Speech Book
  Talk Talk Talk
  Say and Do
  Talk About It

## St. Joseph Institute for the Deaf

See It, Say It, Use It—I, II, III
  Designed to develop vocabulary and parts of speech. May be used
  with older children also.

## Teaching Resources

Associations, Sets 1 and 2
  Designed to develop language and classification skills by matching pairs of functional objects, 50 cards.

Categories
  Develop ability to classify food and animal categories. Seven additional categories are available.

Clark Early Language Program (2½ yrs.—H.S.)
  Uses speech, rebuses, and an optional sign language component
  in a multimodal approach to the acquisition of functional language. Vocabulary, matching, sentence presentations, and expressive language activities are included.

Communication Training Program, Level I
  For the learning of expressive and receptive communication skills
  through establishing prelanguage functions, vocabulary, simple
  syntactic structures, and basic semantic relations. Level 2 and 3
  are available for more advanced individuals (through elementary).

Concept Cards, Sets 1 and 2
  Provide language activities for categorizing objects and expression
  of relationships. Toys, food, clothing, animals, and team sports

are presented in Set 1. Set 2 includes musical instruments, the circus, home appliances, and holidays.

*Functions*
Develops ability to categorize, classify and relate objects. Consists of 14 five-card sets.

*Opposites*
Develops understanding of opposite relationships and words used to describe them. Forty pairs.

*Parts and Wholes*
Illustrates parts and wholes of familiar objects.

*People Places and Things*
Develops association skills and verbal expression. Four sets include occupations, stores, recreation, and sports.

*Positions*
Designed to develop understanding of prepositions and the spatial concepts they represent.

*TR Large Picture Cards, Sets 1, 2, 3*
For development of basic language skills as vocabulary, classification, association, and sentence building.

**Teaching Tools**
Puzzles, books, objects, seals, and musical instruments. A variety of materials for all occasions. Supplies to decorate the classroom, prepare for holidays, and conduct lessons. All used in connection with developing speech and language.

**Western Publishing Co.**

*Developing Language from Experiences: A Preschool Activities Kit.*
Provides activities, information, skills in the areas of vocabulary, sequencing, verb tenses, and using "and."

## PRIMARY SCHOOL LISTINGS

**American Guidance Service**

*Peabody Language Developmental Kits, Levels 1, 2, 3*
Designed to emphasize overall language development and cognitive skills.

*Peabody Articulation Cards*

**Clarke School for the Deaf**
Consonant Chart
Vowel Chart

### Communication Skill Builders

*101 Skill-Building Reference Lists: Language Remediation and Expansion*
The skill-building lists include the sounds of language, the structure of language, meaning of language, thinking with language, production of language, and improvisational stories.

*Gameboards for Speech and Language Development*
Twelve gameboards providing activities for drill and practice in speech and language.

*Peel and Put: Speech and Language Development*
Assortment of colorful and hard-to-find pictures.

### Continental Press, Inc.

*Spirit Masters*
These spirit masters range from basic language skills through advanced skills. They include visual readiness skills, language patterns and usage, basic English, advanced English, parts of speech, punctuation, and capitalization in a progressive ordered series. (Kindergarten through high school).

*Spirit Masters—Phonics, speech sounds, and word analysis skills*
These spirit masters are designed to develop phonics, speech sounds, and word analysis skills (kindergarten through high school).

### Crestwood Company

*Crossword Fun*
Spirit duplicating book to promote vocabulary building.

*Illustrated Speech Sounds Series*
Includes initial, medial, final consonants, blends, vowels, and diphthongs in four spirit duplicating books.

*Word Search Detective*
Designed to improve skills involving word search puzzles.

### Developmental Learning Materials

Cards and Puzzles
Motor Expressive Language Picture Cards, I, II
Open Sequence Cards
Sequential Picture Cards I and II
Perception Puzzles
Same or Different Size Cards
Same or Different Proportion Cards
Spatial Relation Picture Cards
Tangram and Puzzle Cards

Visual Discrimination Matching Cards I, II, III
Visual Memory Cards, I, II, III, IV

### Dormac Incorporated

Apple Tree
A patterned Program of Linguistic Expansion through reinforced experiences and evaluations. A sequential, developmental language program based on linguistics. Six workbooks with pre- and postmeasurements.

Building Sentences Step by Step
A 13-step program for the formation of sentences through the use of verb word cards.

Fun Pages
Supplemental workbooks for the Apple Tree Program. Imaginative adjectives and prepositions designed to promote a generalization of adjectives and prepositions.
Also useful with the Apple Tree language program.

### General Electric, Instructional Industries, Inc.

Project Life-Language Improvement to Facilitate Education
Designed to promote functional language. Programmed instructional filmstrips from prereading level through advanced reading and language levels. Includes a variety of tasks; perceptual training, thinking activities, language and reading, parts of speech, and conceptual skill builders. Student Funbooks, Project Life, Holidayland, and Storyland are also available.

### Ideal School Supply Company

Naming Actions Cards
Naming Names Cards
Sequence Picture Cards
Spatial Relationship Cards

### Instructs/McGraw-Hill

Opposite Concepts
Understanding Our Feelings

### Interstate Printers and Publishers

The Big Book of Language Through Sounds
The Big Book of Sounds
Both are used for practice with speech sounds.

Speech Activity Card File

### Jenn Publications

Language Arts Spirit Masters

Designed to promote reading and language skills for all age levels. Additional supplementary materials are also available.

*Phonic Worksheets*
Designed to stimulate phonic skills.

## The Judy Company

*Judy Puzzles*
An assortment of puzzles covering topics such as animals, occupations, fairy tales, holidays, nursery rhymes, and general religious situations.

## Kenworthy Educational Service, Inc.
Materials for manipulative use—refer to the Developmental Learning Material list and teaching resources list.

## MacMillan Publishing Company, Inc.

*Early Childhood Discovery Materials*
A variety of materials to stimulate understanding and knowledge about common environmental settings. The park, zoo, school, store, clinic, market, farm, and street are included.

## Mafex Associates, Inc.

*Association Cards*
Designed to teach about careers to enhance speech and language.

*Matching Moods*
Designed to promote conversational communication through role playing.

*Story Stimulus Cards*
Designed to stimulate stories about what has happened, what is happening, and what will happen in the cards.

## Milliken Publishing Company

*Look, Listen, and Learn Program*
Designed to develop reading readiness, consonants, vowels, and advanced reading skills.

*Manipulative Activity Card Books*
Reinforces specific phonics skills: long and short vowels, initial consonant digraphs, final consonant digraphs.

## Milton Bradley
Materials for manipulative use—refer to the Developmental Learning Material list and teaching resources list.

## Newby Visualanguage, Inc.
Language arts materials consisting of drawings, worksheets and

workbooks, and flashcards. Basic concepts covered are verbs, pronouns, adjectives, prepositions, idioms, and life concepts such as birth, death, marriage, family, housekeeping, etc.

### *St. Johns School for the Deaf*

Books
Sequencing with Julie, Jack, and Friends
Writing Stories with Julie and Jack

### *Teaching Resources*

*Alike Because, Levels 1 and 2*
Develop association and generalization skills comparing pictures of common objects.

*Developmental Language Lessons, Level 1 and 2*
Designed to teach children basic grammatical structures in a conversational setting. There are eight grammatical categories presented.

*Developmental Syntax Program*
Designed to remediate common syntactical errors; articles; personal pronouns; possessive pronouns; adjectives; "is," "are," "was," "were" verbs; plurality; past tense of regular and irregular verbs; negation; questions; and conjunctions.

*Fokes Sentence Builder*
Develops skills of verbal expression, comprehension, and sentence construction through a structured approach to teaching grammar—who, what, is doing, which, and where are the categories included.

*Fokes Sentence Builder Expansion*
The three additional categories in this supplement are whose, how, and when.

*Additional Sentence Builder Cards*
One hundred eighty picture cards to use with the above program.

*Open-Ended Sequence Cards*
Develops association skills and language expression through the sequencing of a variety of common activities.

*Parts of Speech*
Develps basic parts of speech: nouns, verbs, adjectives, adverbs, and prepositions.

*Sequence Picture Cards, Level 1 and 2*
Develops an understanding of temporal order, events that occur over time, and cause-effect relationships.

*Singulars and Plurals, Sets 1 and 2*
Presentations of singular and plural nouns, both regular and irregular.

*What's Missing, Levels 1 and 2*
Level 1 cards present simple drawings of objects, animals, and people in which details are missing.
Level 2 cards present scenes from which parts are missing.

*What's Wrong Here? Posters on Levels 1 and 2*
Designed to stimulate group discussion on the errors involving the poster scene details.

### Western Publishing Company

*Speaking from Experiences: A Language Interaction Kit*
Provides drill, interaction, and barrier games to develop language. The kit contains books, cards, games, and toys.

## JUNIOR-SENIOR HIGH SCHOOL LISTINGS

### Alexander Graham Bell Association

*Dictionary of Idioms*
Designed as a supplement.

*The Language of Classifications: Animals*
Self-correcting classification program.
Designed to develop the ability to generalize, use deductive reasoning, and understand the use of some, all, both, and either-or.
*The Language of Directions*
Self-correcting format for follow directions.

### Barnell Loft and Dexter Westbrook Publications

*The New Specific Skills Series Working With Sounds*
A progressive 12-level series of sounds produced in the initial, medial, and final position of words. May also be used with elementary school children.

### Bell and Howell Company

*Language Master*
For use with language cards, also made by this company. Several card units available covering words, sentences, parts of speech, vocabulary, and language skills.

### Developmental Learning Materials

Antonymn Cards
Cards and Games
Compound Word Game
Homonym Cards
Homophone Cards
Logic Cards
Photo Sequential Cards
Reaction Cards
Sequential Picture Cards IV

### Dormac Incorporated

*Lessons in Syntax*
Self-correcting lessons designed to stimulate skills in clause and
phrase structure and transformations; included are negative, yes-
no, and "wh" questions, as well as clause transformations.

*Raining Cats and Dogs*
A workbook of idioms divided into categories including meaning,
application, vocabulary, usage, and relating to an experience.

*TSA Syntax Program (Workbooks)*
Self-correcting format focusing on question formation, relativi-
zation, verb processes, and pronominalization.

*VIC Series*
Vocabulary in context to promote the understanding and proper
usage of vocabulary words.

### Gallaudet College

*STEP Series*
Structured Tasks for English Practice workbooks designed for re-
mediable grammatical errors.

### Mafex Associates, Inc.

*Caption Cards*
Designed to stimulate creative writing.

*Dilemma Cards*
Exploration of values and moral reasoning for expressive communication.

*Expressive Language Cards*
Designed for the understanding and use of prepositions and action verbs.

*Milton Bradley*
Antonym Poster Cards
Homonym Poster Cards
Synonym Poster Cards

*St. Johns School for the Deaf*

Books
Building Stories with Julie and Jack
Laugh and Learn with Julie and Jack

*St. Joseph Institute for the Deaf*
Let's Talk
Let's Talk More
Let's Talk More and More


## PUBLISHER'S REFERENCE LIST

Alexander Gram Bell Association for the Deaf, 3417 Volta Place, N.W., Washington, D.C. 20007-2778
American Guidance Service, Publishers' Building, Circle Pines, Minnesota 55014
Barnell Loft, Ltd., 958 Cohruch Street, Baldwin, New York 11510
Bell and Howell Company, Old Mansfield Road, Wooster, Ohio 44691
Bowman/Noble Publishers, Inc., 4563 Colorado Blvd., Los Angeles, CA 90029
Center of Deafness, 600 Waukegan Road, Glenview, IL. 60025
Clarke School for the Deaf, Round Hill Road, Northampton, MA 01060
Communication Skill Builders, 3130 N. Dodge Blvd, P.O. Box 42050-D, Tucson, Arizona 85733
Continental Press, Inc., Elizabethtown, PA 17022
Crestwood Company, 331 South 3rd, St., P.O. Box 04513, Milwaukee, Wisconsin 53204
Developmental Learning Materials, 7440 Natchez Avenue, Niles, IL 60648
Dormac, Inc., P.O. Box 752, Beaverton, Oregon 97075
Gallaudet College, Washington, D.C. 20002
General Electric/Project Life, Instructional Industries, Inc., Executive Park, Ballston Lake, N.Y. 12019
Ideal School Supply Co., 11000 S. Lavergne Ave., Oak Lawn, IL 60453
Instructo/McGraw-Hill, Cecar Hollow and Matthews Rds., Paoli, PA 19301
The Interstate Printers & Publishers, Inc., 19–27 N. Jackson St., Danville, IL 61832
Jenn Publications, P.O. Box 32120, Louisville, KY 40232
The Judy Company, 310 N. Second St., Minneapolis, MN 55401
Kenworthy Educational Services, Inc., P.O. Box 3031, 138 Allen Street, Buffalo, NY 14205
The MacMillan Publishing Company, Inc., Front and Brown Sts.
Mafex Associate, Inc., 90 Cherry Street, Box 519, Johnstown, PA 15907

Milliken Publishing Co., 1100 Research Blvd., St. Louis, MO 63132
Milton Bradley, Educational Division and Playskool Educational Materials, Springfield, MA 01101
Modern Education, P.O. Box 721, Tulsa, OK 74101
Newby Visualanguage Inc., Box 121-A, Eagleville, PA 19408
Rochester Institute of Technology, National Technical Institute for the Deaf, One Lomb Memorial Drive, P.O. Box 9887, Rochester, NY 14623
Society for Visual Education, 1345 Diversey Parkway, Chicago, IL 60614
St. Joseph Institute for the Deaf, 1483–82nd Blvd., St. Louis, MO 63132
St. Johns School for the Deaf, 3680 S. Kinnickinnic Ave., Milwaukee, Wisconsin 53207
Teaching Tools, P.O. Box 27567, Phoenix, Arizona 85061
Teaching Resources Corporation, A New York Times Company, 50 Pond Park Road, Hingham, MA 02043–4382
Western Publishing Co., Inc., Golden Press Division, 1220 Mound Avenue, Racine, WI 53404

## REFERENCE

McCarr, D., & Wisser, M.W. Curriculum materials useful for the hearing impaired. Beaverton, Oregon: Dormae, 1979.

# Index